핵꿀잼 Reading

재밌어서 계속 읽는 중학 영어

LEVEL 1

핵꿀잼 리딩 Level 1

저자 I 타보름 교재 개발팀
디자인 I 디자인 A
일러스트 I 정승원
발행인 I 이선미
발행일 I 개정 4쇄 2024년 1월 10일
발행처 I 타보름 교육
홈페이지 I www.taborm.com

핵꿀잼 Reading

그냥 화끈하게 다 재미있어라!

중등부 학생들과 독해 수업을 하면서 아이들에게 흥미를 불러 일으키는 것들이 어른들의 기준과는 많이 다르다는 것을 느꼈습니다. 쉬어가기로 유머 지문이 드문드문 섞여 있다면 오히려 아이들의 편식을 유발할 수 있습니다. 그렇다면 그냥 화끈하게 다 재미있으면 어떨까? 그렇게해서 수업할 때 반응이 가장 좋았던 소재들을 모아봤습니다. 사랑, 공포, 전설, 감동, 유머, 이야기 등등.

그리고 교양지식까지...!

하지만 '앎'에 대한 욕구는 어린 학생들에게도 있습니다. '아' 다르고 '어' 다르듯이 어떻게 쓰느냐에 따라 지루한 이야기가 될 수도 있고 흥미진진한 이야기가 될 수도 있습니다. 그래서 이후에 지식을 스스로 확장할 수 있게 흥미를 제대로 유발시키기로 했습니다.

학생들이 모든 단어를 알지 못한 채로 독해를 접하게 되고 문맥속에서 자연스럽게 단어의 뜻을 추론하고 해석이 되도록 심혈을 기울였습니다. 모든 문제는 단어 추론, 내용 이해로만 구성이 되어 정말 독해에 푹 빠질 수 있게 설계되었습니다.

– 타보름 교재 개발팀 –

핵꿀잼 Reading 이 특별한 이유

사랑, 공포, 지식, 유머, 심리테스트까지!

독해 욕구 완전 풀 가동

편식 방지!

목차 무작위 구성

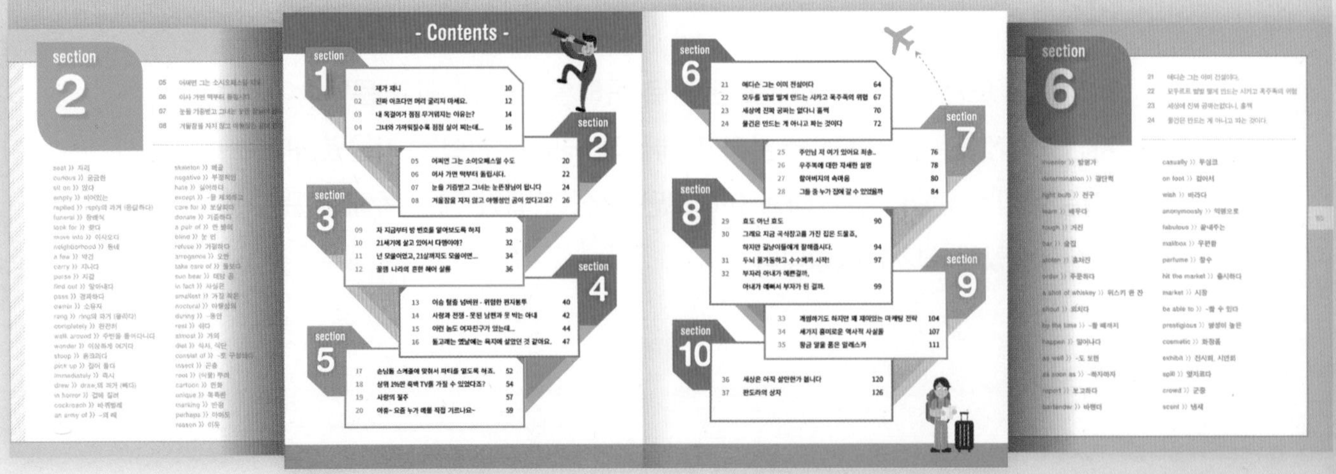

문법 공부는 문법책으로!

내용 이해, 단어 추론 문제로만 구성

독해의 즐거움 뿐만 아니라 깨닫는 즐거움까지!

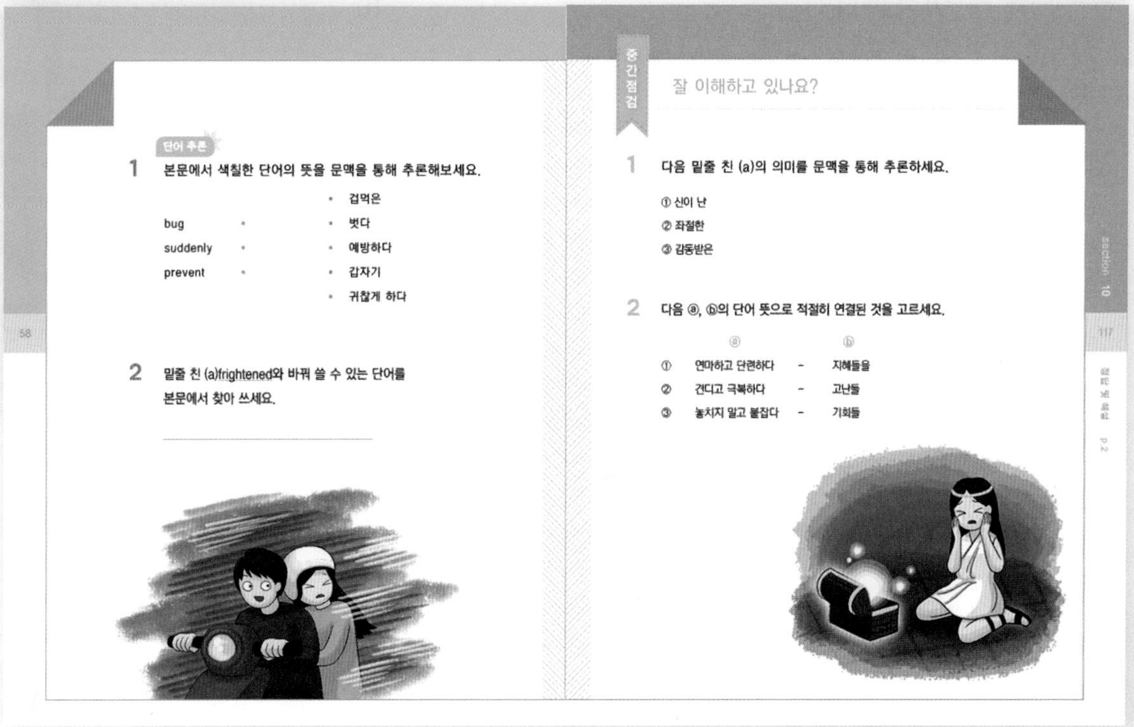
단어 추론

1 본문에서 색칠한 단어의 뜻을 문맥을 통해 추론해보세요.

	• 겁먹은
bug •	• 벗다
suddenly •	• 예방하다
prevent •	• 갑자기
	• 귀찮게 하다

2 밑줄 친 (a)frightened와 바꿔 쓸 수 있는 단어를 본문에서 찾아 쓰세요.

58

중간점검

잘 이해하고 있나요?

1 다음 밑줄 친 (a)의 의미를 문맥을 통해 추론하세요.

① 신이 난
② 좌절한
③ 감동받은

2 다음 ⓐ, ⓑ의 단어 뜻으로 적절히 연결된 것을 고르세요.

	ⓐ		ⓑ
①	연마하고 단련하다	-	지혜들을
②	견디고 극복하다	-	고난들
③	놓치지 말고 붙잡다	-	기회들

section 10

117

정답 및 해설 p.2

좋아, 자연스러웠어!

단문에서 장문으로 서서히 이어지는 독해구성

상상 초월!

풍부한 추가 자료 제공

- Contents -

section 1

grocery 〉〉 식료품

aisle 〉〉 코너, 통로

ask 〉〉 요구하다

began 〉〉 begin의 과거 (시작하다)

scream 〉〉 소리치다

plop down 〉〉 철푸덕 앉다

refuse 〉〉 거절하다

continue 〉〉 지속하다

stood 〉〉 stand의 과거 (서다)

murmur 〉〉 중얼거리다

worry 〉〉 걱정하다

calm 〉〉 침착한

nearby 〉〉 근처에

gentle 〉〉 상냥한

daughter 〉〉 딸

catch a cold 〉〉 감기에 걸리다

while 〉〉 ~동안

answer 〉〉 대답하다

however 〉〉 그러나

charge 〉〉 청구하다

hear 〉〉 듣다

visit 〉〉 방문하다

examine 〉〉 검사하다

glad 〉〉 기쁜

gave 〉〉 give의 과거 (주다)

medicine 〉〉 약

recover 〉〉 회복하다

Popua New Guinea 〉〉 파푸아뉴기니

traditional 〉〉 전통적인

native 〉〉 원주민

necklace 〉〉 목걸이

strange 〉〉 이상한

scary 〉〉 무서운

custom 〉〉 관습

thin 〉〉 날씬한

expensive 〉〉 비싼

delicious 〉〉 맛있는

order 〉〉 주문하다

overcome 〉〉 극복하다

temptation 〉〉 유혹

end up -ing 〉〉 결국 ~하다

not at all 〉〉 전혀

accidentally 〉〉 우연히

heard 〉〉 hear의 과거 (듣다)

01

재가 제니?

A young mother was shopping for groceries with her little girl. When they walked by the candy aisle, the little girl asked her mother for some candy. When the mother said no, the little girl began to scream and cry. ①She plopped down on the ground and refused to move. She continued to scream and cry.

The mother stood next to ②her daughter and ③she started to murmur, “it’s ok, Jenny. It’s ok. Don’t worry. Don’t scream. Don’t cry. Stay calm. Everything’s going to be alright, ④Jenny.” An old woman who was nearby told ⑤her what a gentle mother she was to her little Jenny. The mother said to the woman, “I’m Jenny.”

Words

- grocery
- aisle
- ask
- began
- scream
- plop down
- refuse
- continue
- stood
- daughter
- murmur
- worry
- calm
- nearby
- gentle

단어 추론

1 본문에서 색칠한 단어의 뜻을 문맥을 통해 추론해보세요.

		*	중얼거리다
grocery	*	*	엎드리다
plop down	*	*	털썩 주저앉다
murmur	*	*	식료품
		*	백화점

2 밑줄 친 대상이 가리키는 것이 다른 하나를 고르세요.

① She ② her ③ She ④ Jenny ⑤ her

3 본문에 대한 설명과 일치하지 않는 것을 고르세요.

① 한 모녀가 장을 보고 있었다.
② 엄마의 딸은 사탕을 먹고 싶어했다.
③ 엄마는 사탕을 사주지 않으려 했다.
④ 엄마는 울고 있는 딸을 달래주었다.
⑤ 지나가던 사람이 엄마에게 말을 걸었다.

02

진짜 아프다면
머리 굴리지
마세요.

Jack caught a bad cold while staying at a hotel, so Jack asked the front desk if he knew a nice doctor. The clerk answered, "Of course! I know a nice doctor. However, he charges 30 dollars for the first visit and 10 dollars for the second and third visits."

After hearing that, Jack smiled, because he had an idea. He visited the doctor and said, (a)<u>"Hello, Doctor. I'm here again."</u> The doctor examined Jack for a while. Then, he told Jack, "Jack, I'm glad I gave you some good medicine last time. You had better continue taking it. You will recover soon."

Words

catch a cold
while
answer
however
charge
hear
visit
examine
glad
gave
medicine
recover

단어 추론

1 본문에서 색칠한 단어의 뜻을 문맥을 통해 추론해보세요.

		*	주사
charge	*	*	약
examine	*	*	방문하다
medicine	*	*	검사하다
		*	부과하다

2 본문에서 Jack이 의사에게 밑줄 친 (a)문장처럼 인사한 이유는 무엇인가요?

① 잘 부탁한다는 의미에서

② 진심으로 반가워서

③ 자신을 기억나게 하려고

④ 돈을 적게 내려고

⑤ 귀찮게 하려고

3 본문과 가장 관련이 깊은 속담을 골라보세요.

① 친구 따라 강남 간다.

② 가는 날이 장날이다.

③ 빈 수레가 요란하다.

④ 바늘도둑이 소도둑 된다.

⑤ 뛰는 놈 위에 나는 놈 있다.

03

내 목걸이가
점점 무거워지는
이유는?

Words

Papua New Guinea
traditional
native
necklace
strange
scary
custom

people in Papua New Guinea are still very traditional. Many of the native men of Papua New Guinea are missing fingers. In their tradition, if two young men fight, the winner cuts off a finger from the loser's hand. He then gives the finger to his girlfriend or wife. Then she makes a necklace out of it and wears it on her neck. It is a very strange and scary custom.

단어 추론

1 본문에서 색칠한 단어의 뜻을 문맥을 통해 추론해보세요.

		*	현대적인
traditional	*	*	전통적인
necklace	*	*	귀걸이
strange	*	*	이상한
		*	목걸이

2 다음 문장은 본문의 내용입니다. 빈칸에 알맞은 단어를 본문에서 찾아 쓰세요.

Women in Papua New Guinea are wearing a necklace made of ________________________.

3 파푸아뉴기니에서 만약 당신의 남편이 싸움을 잘한다면 당신이 하고 있을 목걸이를 상상하여 그려보세요.

정답 및 해설 p.2

04

그녀와
가까워질수록
점점 살이 찌는데

Words

- thin
- expensive
- delicious
- order
- overcome
- temptation
- end up -ing
- not at all
- accidentally

My best friend, Celine, is beautiful. She is also thin and tall for her age, but she always wants to lose her weight more. She always talks about being healthy and thin. When we go to a restaurant together, she chooses expensive and delicious food. Then, she says kindly, "I ordered for you, try it! I am so full." Then, (A)<u>I can't overcome the temptation</u>, so I end up eating her food.

Do you know why she is doing this to me? Do you think it's because she is kind and sweet? Not at all! One day, I accidentally heard Celine talking to her friend. She said, "I feel so happy when I see someone get fat." Can you believe that? I really want to kick her.

정답 및 해설 p.3

1 본문에서 알 수 있는 Celine의 성격과 가장 가까운 것을 고르세요.

① friendly ② honest ③ mean
④ unkind ⑤ thoughtful

2 이 글을 쓸 때 주인공의 심경이 어땠을지 추론해보세요.

① happy ② satisfied ③ upset
④ sad ⑤ tired

3 밑줄 친 문장 (A)의 의미를 앞 뒤 문맥을 통해 해석해보세요.

____

4 본문을 읽고 추론할 수 <u>없는</u> 것은 무엇인가요? (2개)

① 주인공과 Celine은 동갑이다.
② Celine은 먹지도 않을 음식을 주문하곤 했다.
③ Celine는 항상 글쓴이를 배려한다.
④ Celine은 날씬한데다 아름답기까지 하다.
⑤ Celine은 자신의 몸무게에 만족하지 못한다.

section 1

Words Test

다음 영어 단어의 뜻을 적으시오.

01	grocery		23	examine	
02	aisle		24	glad	
03	ask		25	gave	
04	began		26	medicine	
05	scream		27	recover	
06	plop down		28	Popua New Guinea	
07	refuse		29	traditional	
08	continue		30	native	
09	stood		31	necklace	
10	murmur		32	strange	
11	worry		33	scary	
12	calm		34	custom	
13	nearby		35	thin	
14	gentle		36	expensive	
15	daughter		37	delicious	
16	catch a cold		38	order	
17	while		39	overcome	
18	answer		40	temptation	
19	however		41	end up -ing	
20	charge		42	not at all	
21	hear		43	accidentally	
22	visit		44	heard	

section 2

05 어쩌면 그는 소시오패스일지도

06 이사 가면 떡부터 돌립시다.

07 눈을 기증받고 그녀는 눈뜬 장님이 됩니다.

08 겨울잠을 자지 않고 야행성인 곰이 있다고요?

seat 〉〉 자리
curious 〉〉 궁금한
sit on 〉〉 앉다
empty 〉〉 비어있는
replied 〉〉 reply의 과거 (응답하다)
funeral 〉〉 장례식
look for 〉〉 찾다
move into 〉〉 이사오다
neighborhood 〉〉 동네
a few 〉〉 약간
carry 〉〉 지니다
purse 〉〉 지갑
find out 〉〉 알아내다
pass 〉〉 경과하다
owner 〉〉 소유자, 주인
rang 〉〉 ring의 과거 (울리다)
completely 〉〉 완전히
walk around 〉〉 주변을 돌아다니다
wonder 〉〉 이상하게 여기다
stoop 〉〉 웅크리다
pick up 〉〉 집어 들다
immediately 〉〉 즉시
drew 〉〉 draw의 과거 (빼다)
in horror 〉〉 겁에 질려
cockroach 〉〉 바퀴벌레
an army of 〉〉 ~의 떼

skeleton 〉〉 해골
negative 〉〉 부정적인
hate 〉〉 싫어하다
except 〉〉 ~을 제외하고
care for 〉〉 보살피다
donate 〉〉 기증하다
a pair of 〉〉 한 쌍의
blind 〉〉 눈 먼
refuse 〉〉 거절하다
arrogance 〉〉 오만
take care of 〉〉 돌보다
sun bear 〉〉 태양 곰
in fact 〉〉 사실은
smallest 〉〉 가장 작은
noctural 〉〉 야행성의
during 〉〉 ~동안
rest 〉〉 쉬다
almost 〉〉 거의
diet 〉〉 식사, 식단
consist of 〉〉 ~로 구성되다
insect 〉〉 곤충
root 〉〉 (식물) 뿌리
cartoon 〉〉 만화
unique 〉〉 독특한
marking 〉〉 반점
perhaps 〉〉 아마도
reason 〉〉 이유

05

어쩌면 그는
소시오패스
일지도

Words

look for
seat
curious
sit on
empty
replied
funeral

Joe was at a baseball game. When he was looking for his seat, he saw that a man was sitting on a seat and he put his bag and coat on another seat. Joe became curious. He asked the man why he had bought two tickets. The man replied that the empty seat was for his wife, but she was dead.

Hearing the answer, Joe felt so sorry for him, but he asked the man why he didn't give the empty seat to any of his family members or relatives. He replied, "I tried, but (a)<u>they</u> all went to my wife's funeral."

단어 추론

1 본문에서 색칠한 단어의 뜻을 문맥을 통해 추론해보세요.

		* 결혼식
curious	*	* 비어있는
empty	*	* 궁금한
funeral	*	* 장례식
		* 무관심한

2 밑줄 친 (a)<u>they</u>가 가리키는 것을 본문에서 찾아 영어로 쓰세요.

____

3 남자의 마지막 말을 들은 Joe의 심경이 어땠을지 추론해보세요.

① sad ② sympathetic ③ moved
④ confused ⑤ funny

4 본문의 남자에 대해 알 수 <u>없는</u> 것은 무엇인가요?

① 남자는 아내가 죽고 큰 슬픔에 잠겼다.
② 남자는 혼자서 야구 경기에 갔다.
③ 남자는 한 자리에 가방과 코트만을 뒀다.
④ 남자는 아내의 장례식에 가지 않았다.
⑤ 남자는 남는 티켓을 다른 사람에게 주려고 했다.

06

이사 가면
떡부터
돌립시다

In Japan, a young woman and her baby moved into a house. They were new to the neighborhood, so they did not know anyone. A few days after moving in, the mother was killed in a car accident. Because she was not carrying her purse at that time, no one could find out who she was.

A few months passed. The owner of the mother's house came and rang the bell. There was no answer. After waiting a while, he opened the door with his own key. The house was completely dark. He walked around calling the young mother's name. In the living room, he stopped. There was a small black doll on the floor. The man wondered why the doll was there. He stooped to pick it up, but immediately drew his hand back in horror. It was no black doll. It was an army of cockroaches on a skeleton of a human baby.

Words

- move into
- neighborhood
- a few
- carry
- purse
- find out
- owner
- rang
- completely
- walk around
- wonder
- stoop
- pick up
- immediately
- drew
- in horrror
- cockroaches
- an army of
- skeleton

단어 추론

1 본문에서 색칠한 단어의 뜻을 문맥을 통해 추론해보세요.

		*	동네
neighborhood	*	*	이웃
accident	*	*	사고
skeleton	*	*	해골
		*	귀신

2 다음 문장은 본문의 내용입니다. 빈칸에 알맞은 단어를 본문에서 찾아 쓰세요.

Finally, the house owner found the baby covered with a swarm of ________________.

3 본문에 대한 설명과 일치하지 않는 것을 고르세요.

① 새로운 동네에서 젊은 엄마와 아기를 아는 사람이 거의 없었다.

② 젊은 엄마는 교통사고로 죽었다.

③ 엄마가 죽었을 당시 신원이 밝혀지지 않았다.

④ 엄마가 죽고 이후에 아기는 해골이 된 채 발견됐다.

⑤ 집주인이 발견한 것은 인형이 아니었다.

07

눈을 기증 받고
그녀는
눈뜬 장님이
됩니다

Words

- negative
- hate
- except
- care for
- donate
- a pair of
- blind
- refuse
- arrogance
- take care of

There was a girl who was unhappy, because she was blind. She was always negative. She hates everything and everyone except her boyfriend. Her boyfriend was always with her and cared for her so much. One day, he asked her to marry him. But, she said, “If I could see the world, I would marry you.”

Time passed, someone donated a pair of eyes to her, and so she came to see everything. Again, her boyfriend asked her to marry him. When she looked at him, she could know that he was blind, too. She refused with arrogance. He sadly walked away and later left a short message to her: “Just take care of my eyes, darling.”

단어 추론

1 본문에서 색칠한 단어의 뜻을 문맥을 통해 추론해보세요.

		*	긍정적인
negative	*	*	기증하다
donate	*	*	오만함
arrogance	*	*	감동
		*	부정적인

2 다음 문장은 본문의 내용입니다. 빈칸에 알맞은 단어를 본문에서 찾아 쓰세요.

Actually, someone who donated her the eyes was her ______________________.

3 본문의 장님인 소녀에 대해 알 수 없는 것은 무엇인가요?

① 항상 부정적이었다.
② 결국 시력을 되찾게 된다.
③ 장님인 소녀의 남자친구도 원래 장님이었다.
④ 남자친구는 소녀를 매우 사랑했다.
⑤ 남자친구와 결국 헤어졌다.

08

겨울잠을
자지 않고
야행성인 곰이
있다고요?

Words

- sun bear
- in fact
- smallest
- nocturnal
- during
- rest
- almost
- diet
- consist of
- insect
- root
- cartoon
- unique
- marking
- perhaps
- reason

Bears are usually very big. However, some bears are small. The sun bear is a small bear. In fact, ①it is the smallest kind of bear. Sun bears are (a)nocturnal: they are usually active at night. During the day, they rest on trees. They can eat almost anything. Their diet (b)consists of insects, fruits, roots, birds, and other small animals. Like bears in cartoons, sun bears love honey. Sun bears have a unique marking on them that looks like a rising sun. Perhaps that is the reason why they are called sun bears.

1 본문에서 밑줄 친 단어 (a), (b)의 뜻을 문맥을 통해 추론해보세요.

(a) ________________

(b) ________________

2 본문에서 밑줄 친 ①it이 가리키는 것이 무엇인지 한글로 적으세요.

____

3 본문의 태양곰에 대한 설명으로 알맞은 것을 고르세요.

① 태양곰은 겨울잠을 오래 잔다.

② 태양곰은 주로 낮에 활동하는 것을 좋아한다.

③ 태양곰은 거의 아무거나 잘 먹는다.

④ 태양곰은 만화에 나오는 곰들처럼 꿀을 좋아하진 않는다.

⑤ 태양을 좋아하는 습성 때문에 태양곰이라 이름 지어졌다.

정답 및 해설 p.6

section 2

Words Test

다음 영어 단어의 뜻을 적으시오.

01	seat		28	negative	
02	curious		29	hate	
03	sit on		30	except	
04	empty		31	care for	
05	replied		32	donate	
06	funeral		33	a pair of	
07	look for		34	blind	
08	move into		35	refuse	
09	neighborhood		36	arrogance	
10	a few		37	take care of	
11	carry		38	sun bear	
12	purse		39	in fact	
13	find out		40	smallest	
14	pass		41	nocturnal	
15	owner		42	during	
16	rang		43	rest	
17	completely		44	almost	
18	walk around		45	diet	
19	wonder		46	consist of	
20	stoop		47	insect	
21	pick up		48	root	
22	immediately		49	cartoon	
23	drew		50	unique	
24	in horror		51	marking	
25	cockroach		52	perhaps	
26	an army of		53	reason	
27	skeleton				

section 3

just before 〉〉 바로 전에
fall asleep 〉〉 잠들다
realize 〉〉 깨닫다
parking lot 〉〉 주차장
stuff 〉〉 물건
lock 〉〉 잠그다
only 〉〉 단지
remember 〉〉 기억하다
for a while 〉〉 잠시
unlock 〉〉 열다
honk 〉〉 울리다
horn 〉〉 경적
turn on 〉〉 켜다
law 〉〉 법
make sense 〉〉 타당하다
example 〉〉 예
past 〉〉 과거
strange 〉〉 이상한
century 〉〉 세기
on purpose 〉〉 일부러
build 〉〉 짓다
have to 〉〉 ~해야만 한다
pay 〉〉 지불하다
tax 〉〉 세금
female 〉〉 여성
allow 〉〉 허용하다
get into 〉〉 ~을 (시작)하다
relationship 〉〉 (연인) 관계

date 〉〉 데이트하다
be fired 〉〉 해고 당하다
get out 〉〉 나가다
fairy 〉〉 요정
become 〉〉 ~이 되다
curse 〉〉 저주하다
beast 〉〉 짐승
once upon a time 〉〉 옛날 옛날에
far away 〉〉 아주 먼
castle 〉〉 성
arrogant 〉〉 오만한
knock 〉〉 두드리다
beg 〉〉 구걸하다
stay 〉〉 머물다
until 〉〉 ~때까지
someone 〉〉 누군가
truly 〉〉 진정으로
remain 〉〉 남다
refuse 〉〉 거부하다
hair salon 〉〉 미용실
wait 〉〉 기다리다
hairdresser 〉〉 미용사
come back 〉〉 돌아오다
excellent 〉〉 훌륭한
forgot 〉〉 forget의 과거 (잊다)
met 〉〉 meet의 과거 (만나다)
grab 〉〉 붙잡다

09

Two friends couldn't hear well. They were traveling together. As it grew dark, they came to a hotel. Just before he fell asleep, one of the friends realized that he had left something in the car. He went out to the parking lot and to his car. After getting his stuff, he locked the car, only to realize that he didn't remember his room number.

After thinking for a while, he had an idea. He unlocked the car, sat in the driver's seat, and started (a)<u>honking the horn</u>. Soon, every room in the hotel started turning on its lights. Every room did, except for one.

자, 지금부터
방 번호를
알아보도록 하지

Words

just before
fell asleep
realize
parking lot
stuff
lock
only
remember
for a while
unlock
honk
horn
turn on

단어 추론

1 본문에서 색칠한 단어의 뜻을 문맥을 통해 추론해보세요.

		*	남겨두다
realize	*	*	기억하다
parking lot	*	*	깨닫다
remember	*	*	놀이터
		*	주차장

2 본문에서 밑줄 친 표현 (a)의 뜻을 문맥을 통해 추론해보세요.

3 다음 중 본문의 제목으로 적절한 것을 고르세요.

① the way we sleep well

② the way we help a person who can't hear well

③ the way we park a car better

④ the way a person who can't hear well finds his room

⑤ the way we remember well

10

21세기에
살고 있어서
다행이야

Laws don't always make sense. These are some examples of strange laws in the past.

During the 18th century in England, poor people lived in houses without any windows on purpose. They didn't build windows because they had to pay taxes for every window in their house. If you go to the British countryside, you can still see houses without windows.

During the 19th century in America, female teachers were not allowed to get into a relationship. If they chose to marry or date, they would be fired.

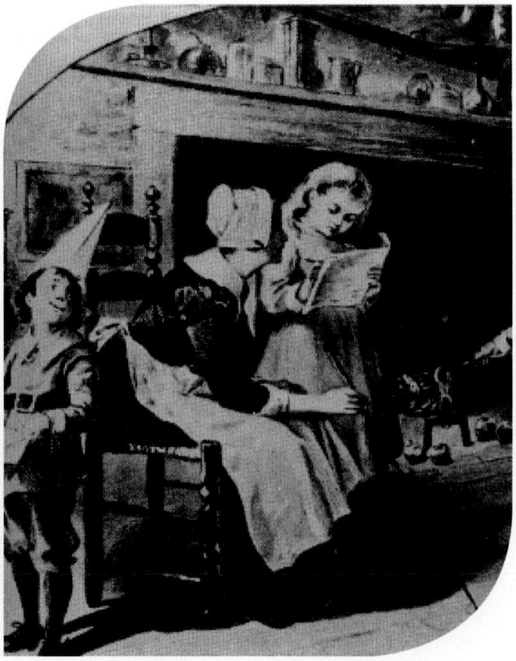

Words

- law
- make sense
- example
- in the past
- strange
- century
- purpose
- build
- have to
- pay
- tax
- female
- allow
- get into
- relationship
- date
- be fired

단어 추론

1 본문에서 색칠한 단어의 뜻을 문맥을 통해 추론해보세요.

		*	사귀다
strange	*	*	이상한
tax	*	*	허락하다
allow	*	*	세금
		*	해고하다

2 다음은 본문의 내용입니다. 빈칸에 알맞은 말을 한글로 써넣으세요.

(a) 18세기 영국에서 창문 없는 집들이 있었다.
왜냐하면 ______________________________.

(b) 19세기 미국에서 여자 교사들은
______________________________ 것이 불법이었다.

11

넌
모쓸이었고
21살까지
모쓸이면...

Words

get out
fairy
became
curse
beast
Once upon a time
far away
castle
arrogant
knock
beg
a place to stay
gave
until
someone
truly
would
remain
refuse

(A) But, the prince refused and told her to get out. The old woman then became a fairy. She then cursed the prince by turning him into a beast.

(B) Once upon a time, in a kingdom far, far away, there was a beautiful castle on the top of a mountain. In the castle lived a young, handsome prince who was very arrogant. One very cold night, an old and poor woman knocked the castle door. She begged the young prince for a place to stay during the night.

(C) She gave him a rose and told him that the rose would live until the prince's twenty first birthday. If he did not find someone who loves him truly by then, he would remain as a beast until the day he died.

단어 추론

1 본문에서 색칠한 단어의 뜻을 문맥을 통해 추론해보세요.

		*	꾸미다
refuse	*	*	구걸하다
arrogant	*	*	오만한
beg	*	*	저주하다
		*	거절하다

2 본문을 순서대로 배열하세요.

__________ → __________ → __________

3 본문에 대한 설명과 일치하지 <u>않는</u> 것을 고르세요.

① 왕자는 산꼭대기에 있는 아름다운 성에 살았다.

② 나이든 여자는 사실은 요정이었다.

③ 왕자는 잘생겼지만 오만했다.

④ 여자는 왕자를 야수로 변하게 했다.

⑤ 왕자는 잘못을 뉘우칠 때까지 야수로 살아야 한다.

12

꿀잼 나라의 흔한
헤어 살롱

A man and a boy walked into a hair salon. The boy waited while the man got a haircut first. After he was done, the man took the boy and sat him on a chair. The man asked the hairdresser to give the boy a good haircut. Then, he told the boy that he would come back after making a few phone calls. The hairdresser gave the boy an excellent haircut. However, the man did not return.

After waiting for his return for a long time, the hairdresser said to the boy, "I think your father forgot about you. I am a little worried about him." But, the boy replied, "(a)<u>He</u> is not my father. We met this morning. He grabbed my hand, and told me that we were going to get a free haircut.

Words

- hair salon
- wait
- hairdresser
- come back
- excellent
- forgot
- worry about
- met
- grab

1 밑줄 친 (a)가 누군지 골라보세요.

① man ② boy ③ hairdresser

2 본문에 대한 설명과 일치하는 것을 고르세요.

① 소년은 아빠와 미용실에 갔다.
② 소년이 남자보다 먼저 머리를 했다.
③ 남자는 잠시 전화를 하고 돌아왔다.
④ 소년과 남자의 머리 비용이 많이 나왔다.
⑤ 소년과 남자는 오늘 처음 만난 사이였다.

3 소년의 마지막 말을 들은 미용사의 심경이 어땠을지 추론해보세요.

① upset
② excited
③ happy
④ fun
⑤ satisfied

4 만약 당신이 미용사라면 소년의 말을 듣고 어떤 조치를 취할지 자유롭게 한글로 쓰세요.

section 3

Words Test

다음 영어 단어의 뜻을 적으시오.

01	just before		29	date	
02	fell asleep		30	be fired	
03	realize		31	get out	
04	parking lot		32	fairy	
05	stuff		33	become	
06	lock		34	curse	
07	only		35	beast	
08	remember		36	once upon a time	
09	for a while		37	far away	
10	unlock		38	castle	
11	honk		39	arrogant	
12	horn		40	knock	
13	turn on		41	beg	
14	law		42	stay	
15	make sense		43	until	
16	example		44	someone	
17	past		45	truly	
18	strange		46	remain	
19	century		47	refuse	
20	on purpose		48	hair salon	
21	build		49	wait	
22	have to		50	hairdresser	
23	pay		51	come back	
24	tax		52	excellent	
25	female		53	forgot	
26	allow		54	met	
27	get into		55	grab	
28	relationship				

section 4

post office 〉〉 우체국
grand parrent 〉〉 조부모
envelope 〉〉 봉투
glue 〉〉 풀
lick 〉〉 핥다
shut 〉〉 닫다
tight 〉〉 단단한
brush 〉〉 닦다
lump 〉〉 혹
tongue 〉〉 혀
hurt 〉〉 아프다
examine 〉〉 검사하다
cockroach 〉〉 바퀴벌레
climb out 〉〉 기어나오다
cut open 〉〉 절개하다
enter 〉〉 들어가다
warm 〉〉 따뜻한
moist 〉〉 촉촉한
hatch 〉〉 부화시키다
temper 〉〉 기질
beat 〉〉 때리다
drunk 〉〉 취한
regret 〉〉 후회하다
realize 〉〉 깨닫다
last longer 〉〉 오래 지속되다
forgiveness 〉〉 용서
whenever 〉〉 ~할 때마다
hammer 〉〉 망치질하다
nail 〉〉 못
living room 〉〉 거실
decide 〉〉 결심하다
suggest 〉〉 제안하다
agree 〉〉 동의하다
as time went by 〉〉 시간이 지남에 따라
disappear 〉〉 사라지다
leave 〉〉 떠나다
shock 〉〉 충격을 주다
thought 〉〉 think의 과거 (생각하다)
look at 〉〉 보다
even though 〉〉 ~에도 불구하고
remove 〉〉 제거하다
wound 〉〉 상처
bump 〉〉 쿵!
flat tire 〉〉 바람 빠진 타이어
pull over 〉〉 길 한쪽에 차를 대다
driving 〉〉 운전
sympathetic 〉〉 동조하는
terrible 〉〉 끔찍한
actually 〉〉 실제로
wrong 〉〉 잘못된
dolphin 〉〉 돌고래
gill 〉〉 아가미
breathe 〉〉 호흡하다
underwater 〉〉 물속에서
tail 〉〉 꼬리
leap 〉〉 치솟다
definitely 〉〉 분명히

13

이승 탈출
넘버원
|
위험한
편지 봉투

Words

- post office
- grandparent
- envelope
- glue
- lick
- shut
- tight
- brush
- lump
- tongue
- hurt
- examine
- cockroach
- climb out
- cut open
- enter
- warm
- moist
- hatch

A young man was at a post office. He wrote a letter to his grandparents who lived far away. He put his letter in an envelope, but he didn't have any glue. He licked the envelope and shut it tight. A few days after he sent the letter, he was brushing his teeth when he saw a lump on his tongue. As it began to hurt, he went to the doctor the next day.

After examining him, the doctor cut open the lump, and a cockroach climbed out. The part of the envelope had cockroach eggs. When he licked the envelope, he cut his tongue, and so the eggs entered his tongue. Because it was warm and moist, the eggs could hatch inside his tongue and grew in size. That's why you should always be careful!

단어 추론

1 본문에서 색칠한 단어의 뜻을 문맥을 통해 추론해보세요.

		*	혹
lick	*	*	부화하다
lump	*	*	멍
hatch	*	*	자라다
		*	핥다

2 젊은 남자의 혀에 생긴 혹은 결국 무엇이었는지 한글로 쓰세요.

____

3 본문과 관련된 질문에 대답하기 위해 빈칸에 알맞은 단어를 쓰세요.

Question : How could the cockroach eggs hatch and grow inside his tongue?

Answer : Because it was ____________ and ____________.

정답 및 해설 p.10

14

사랑과 전쟁

|

못된 남편과

못 박는 아내

Words

- temper
- beat
- drunk
- regret
- realize
- last longer
- forgiveness
- whenever
- hammer
- nail
- living room
- decide
- suggest
- agree
- as time went by
- disappear
- leave
- shock
- thought
- look at
- even though
- remove
- wound

Peter had bad tempers. He got angry easily. He even beat his wife when he was drunk. The day after he lost his control, he always regretted and realized how foolish he was. But, it didn't last longer.

One morning, his wife was crying while he was begging for her forgiveness. She said to him, "Whenever you lose your control, I'll hammer a nail on the wall in the living room."

For a month, she hammered twenty eight nails. He finally realized how ugly the living room was. So, he decided to change and he did change. She hammered less and less every day.

Finally, Peter didn't lose his temper at all. He even suggested to his wife that if he did something good to her, she would pull out the nails one by one. She agreed.

As time went by, the nails on the wall disappeared. But, one day, she said to him, “I’m leaving you, take care, Peter.” He was shocked. “Oh, no, darling, I thought I did well. I am different now, you know well.” “That’s right, Peter. But, look at the wall. Even though every nail (a)was removed, the wounds are still there.” she replied.

단어 추론

1 본문에서 색칠한 단어의 뜻을 문맥을 통해 추론해보세요.

		*	떠나다
regret	*	*	지속되다
last	*	*	사라지다
hammer	*	*	후회하다
		*	망치질하다

2 밑줄 친 (a)was removed와 바꿔 쓸 수 있는 한 단어를 본문에서 찾아 쓰세요.

3 모든 못이 제거되었음에도 불구하고 아내가 떠나려는 이유는 무엇인가요?

4 본문에 대한 설명과 일치하지 않는 것을 고르세요.

① Peter는 술을 마시면 아내를 때리기도 했다.

② 그는 이성을 잃은 다음 날이면 후회하곤 했다.

③ 한 달 동안 아내는 벽에 못을 28개 박았다.

④ 노력을 거듭한 후에 벽에 못이 사라졌다.

⑤ 그가 더 이상 이성을 잃지 않자 아내와 행복해졌다.

정답 및 해설 p.11

15

이런 놈도
여자친구가
있는데...

A man was late to a date with his girlfriend. He told her there was a reason why he was late. “I was driving over here when I heard a big ‘POP’, then a bump, bump, bump sound. I knew right away that I had a flat tire. So, I pulled over to the side of the road and changed the tire. However, when I started driving, I started hearing the bump, bump sound again!” His girlfriend was sympathetic. “That road must have been terrible. Your car got another flat tire?” “Actually, no.” the man replied. “I just changed the wrong tire.”

Words

- bump
- flat tire
- pull over
- driving
- sympathetic
- terrible
- actually
- wrong

1 밑줄 친 단어 sympathetic의 뜻을 문맥을 통해 추론해보세요.

① 감동받은

② 기분 나쁜

③ 동조하는

④ 짜증난

⑤ 우울한

2 여자 친구는 타이어를 교체했음에도 쿵쿵 소리가 난 원인이 뭐라고 생각했나요?

① 타이어

② 남자친구

③ 도로

④ 운전실수

⑤ 날씨

3 타이어를 교체했음에도 쿵쿵 소리가 또 난 이유를 한글로 적으세요.

16

돌고래는
옛날에는
육지에서
살았던 것
같아요

Words

dolphin
gill
breathe
underwater
tail
leap
definitely

Some people think that dolphins are fish, but they are actually quite different from fish. Fish have gills to breathe underwater, but dolphins don't have gills. Instead, dolphins need to breathe air like human beings do. Also, when fish swim, they swing their tails from left to right, but a dolphin moves its tail up and down. A dolphin uses its tail to leap high into the air. Dolphins are definitely not fish, even though they may look like them.

1 다음 문장은 본문의 내용입니다. 빈칸에 알맞은 단어를 본문에서 찾아 쓰세요.

Because fish have ______________, they can breathe underwater.

2 본문에 대한 설명과 일치하지 않는 것을 고르세요.

① 돌고래는 아가미로 숨을 쉬지 않는다.

② 돌고래는 사람과 숨쉬는 방식이 똑같다.

③ 물고기는 꼬리를 좌우로 흔든다.

④ 돌고래는 꼬리를 위아래로 흔든다.

⑤ 돌고래도 물고기의 한 종류이다.

Words Test

다음 영어 단어의 뜻을 적으시오.

01	post office		30	living room	
02	grandparent		31	decide	
03	envelope		32	suggest	
04	glue		33	agree	
05	lick		34	as time went by	
06	shut		35	disappear	
07	tight		36	leave	
08	brush		37	shock	
09	lump		38	thought	
10	tongue		39	look at	
11	hurt		40	even though	
12	examine		41	remove	
13	cockroach		42	wound	
14	climb out		43	bump	
15	cut open		44	flat tire	
16	enter		45	pull over	
17	warm		46	driving	
18	moist		47	sympathetic	
19	hatch		48	terrible	
20	temper		49	actually	
21	beat		50	wrong	
22	drunk		51	dolphin	
23	regret		52	gill	
24	realize		53	breathe	
25	last longer		54	underwater	
26	forgiveness		55	tail	
27	whenever		56	leap	
28	hammer		57	definitely	
29	nail				

section 5

husband 〉〉 남편

invite 〉〉 초대하다

force 〉〉 강요하다

unfortunate 〉〉 유감스러운

fortunate 〉〉 운이 좋은

amazing 〉〉 놀라운

invent 〉〉 발명하다

show 〉〉 보여주다

air 〉〉 방송하다

develop 〉〉 발달하다

sold 〉〉 sell의 과거분사 (팔다)

nowadays 〉〉 오늘날

high-definition 〉〉 고화질

frightened 〉〉 무서운

slow down 〉〉 늦추다

moreover 〉〉 게다가

take off 〉〉 벗다

put ~ on 〉〉 입다, 쓰다

bug 〉〉 귀찮게 하다

burst into 〉〉 ~을 터뜨리다

highway 〉〉 고속도로

prevent 〉〉 예방하다

instead of 〉〉 대신에

hand over 〉〉 건네다

discuss 〉〉 의논하다

decide 〉〉 결심하다

farm 〉〉 농사짓다

adorable 〉〉 사랑스러운

send 〉〉 보내다

17

손님들 스케줄에
맞춰서 파티를
열도록 하죠

Words

husband
invite
force
unfortunate
fortunate
amazing

A woman asked her husband to call her friends to their house for a party. The husband didn't want to invite his wife's friends, but his wife forced him to call them anyway. He asked his wife's friends what they were doing tomorrow. They told him they would be free. He then asked what they were doing the next day. They said they would be free that day as well. He then asked what they were doing the day after that, to which they replied that they would be going on a trip. The man then said, "Oh no! That's very ______________! I was going to invite you to our house on that day!"

1 본문의 밑줄 친 빈칸에 들어갈 단어로 알맞은 것을 고르세요.

① happy ② unfortunate ③ fortunate

④ amazing ⑤ lucky

2 본문과 관련된 질문에 대답하기 위해 빈칸에 공통으로 들어갈 단어를 쓰세요.

Question : What was his plan not to invite his wife' s friends?

Answer : His plan was to keep asking if they would be _____________ until they wouldn' t be _____________.

3 본문을 읽고 추론할 수 없는 것은 무엇인가요?

① 남편은 아내의 친구들은 내일 한가할 것이다.

② 남편은 아내의 친구들을 초대하고 싶지 않았다.

③ 남편은 아내의 친구들을 초대하지 않으려고 노력했다.

④ 남편은 아내의 친구들한테 본인의 생각을 솔직히 말하지 않았다.

⑤ 남편이 초대하려고 한 날과 친구들의 스케줄이 우연히 겹쳤다.

18

상위 1%만
흑백 TV를
가질 수
있었다죠?

Words

- invent
- show
- air
- develop
- sold
- nowadays
- high-definition

The first TV was invented in 1925 by John Baird. This had only one color. It is about the size of a human face.

The first TV station was set up in New York in 1928. Only a few people had TVs. In 1928, TVs only showed shows for two hours a day.

By 1948 in America, there were 4 big TV networks. They aired shows 3 hours a day, from 8 to 11 o'clock at night. TVs were not always showing something like it does today.

In 1953, color TVs were finally developed and sold. However, they were often too expensive for most people. Shows were still shown in black and white.

Nowadays most TVs can be watched in (a)<u>high-definition</u>. It means that TVs have many lines, so they can show lots of colors and clear images. Some people even have 3-D TVs (TV's that show video in 3-D) at home.

단어 추론

1 본문에서 색칠한 단어의 뜻을 문맥을 통해 추론해보세요.

		*	방송하다
invent	*	*	발명하다
air	*	*	팔다
expensive	*	*	비싼
		*	보여주다

2 본문에서 밑줄 친 단어 (a)high-definition의 뜻을 문맥을 통해 추론해보세요.

____

3 본문에 나온 TV에 대한 설명으로 알맞지 않은 것을 고르세요. (2개)

① TV는 1928년에 처음으로 발명되었다.

② 하루에 2시간만 방영될 때도 있었다.

③ 컬러 TV가 처음 나온 것은 1953년이었다.

④ 1953년에 컬러 TV가 개발되긴 했지만 판매되진 않았다.

⑤ 라인을 많이 가진 TV일수록 화질이 좋다.

정답 및 해설 p.13

19

Words

- frightened
- slow down
- moreover
- take off
- put ~ on
- bug
- burst into
- highway
- prevent
- instead of
- hand over

A young couple was on a motorcycle. They were going very fast, so the young lady was (a)<u>frightened</u>. Her boyfriend was driving the motorcycle. She asked him to slow down. But, he said he did not want to do so, because driving fast was very fun.

Moreover, he asked her to take off his helmet and put it on her head, because it bugged him so much. He promised her that if she did that, he would slow down. So, she took off his helmet and put it on her head, but he didn't slow down at all. Finally, she got much scared and burst into tears. But, he still didn't slow down. He just told her to love her so much and remember this.

On the evening news that day, there was a motorcycle accident that had happened on the highway. The brakes on the young couple's motorcycle suddenly stopped working. The young man knew that he could not prevent an accident. He had chosen to save his girlfriend instead of himself but, he didn't want to let her know, so he handed over the helmet he wore and told her that he loved her so much.

단어 추론

1 본문에서 색칠한 단어의 뜻을 문맥을 통해 추론해보세요.

		*	겁먹은
bug	*	*	벗다
suddenly	*	*	예방하다
prevent	*	*	갑자기
		*	귀찮게 하다

2 밑줄 친 (a)frightened와 바꿔 쓸 수 있는 단어를 본문에서 찾아 쓰세요.

____

3 본문에 대한 설명과 일치하지 않는 것을 고르세요.

① 고속도로에서 오토바이 사고가 났다.

② 커플이 탄 오토바이의 브레이크 장치가 고장 났다.

③ 남자는 여자친구에게 헬멧을 양보했다.

④ 남자도 오토바이가 고장 났다는 사실을 몰랐다.

⑤ 여자는 남자가 속도를 낮추지 않아 무서웠다.

4 다음 중 본문의 제목으로 적절한 것을 고르세요.

① The importance of safe driving

② The reason why we should wear a motorcycle helmet

③ Love stronger than death

④ How to deal with brake problems

⑤ How to express your love to your girlfriend

20

아휴~

요즘 누가 애를

직접 기르나요~

Words

- discuss
- decide
- farm
- adorable
- send

A little boy and a little girl told the boy's father that they were going to get married. The father asked his son where he and his wife would live. The boy said that he and his future wife had already discussed the matter, and that they had decided that they would make the tree house in the hills.

The boy's father then asked how they would get money to buy food and water. The boy again said that he and his future wife had already discussed the matter, and that they were planning on farming near their tree house, so they wouldn't need much money.

Feeling adorable, the boy's father asked if they would have any children. The boy answered that they were also planning on having children, and that once they had them, they would send their children to their grandparents.

단어 추론

1 본문에서 색칠한 단어의 뜻을 문맥을 통해 추론해보세요.

		*	의논하다
discuss	*	*	사랑스러운
decide	*	*	계획하다
adorable	*	*	결심하다
		*	짜증나게 하는

2 본문을 읽고 추론할 수 <u>없는</u> 것은 무엇인가요?

① 소년과 소녀는 결혼하기로 합의했다.

② 그들은 아이를 직접 키울 계획이다.

③ 그들은 언덕에서 살 계획이다.

④ 그들은 직접 농사를 지을 계획이다.

⑤ 그들은 돈이 많이 필요치 않을 것이라고 생각한다.

3 당신이 아버지였다면 아들의 마지막 말에 뭐라고 반응했을지 한글로 자유롭게 쓰세요.

4 다음은 본문의 내용을 대화체로 쓴 것입니다. 빈칸에 알맞은 단어를 쓰세요.

Father : Where are you going to live?

Boy : We will live in our ______________ house in the hills.

Father : How can you get food?

Boy : We will ______________ near our house.

Father : How can you bring up your children?

Boy : We will send them to their ______________.

section 5

Words Test

다음 영어 단어의 뜻을 적으시오.

01	husband		16	moreover	
02	invite		17	take off	
03	force		18	put ~ on	
04	unfortunate		19	bug	
05	fortunate		20	burst into	
06	amazing		21	highway	
07	invent		22	prevent	
08	show		23	instead of	
09	air		24	hand over	
10	develop		25	discuss	
11	sold		26	decide	
12	nowadays		27	farm	
13	high-definition		28	adorable	
14	frightened		29	send	
15	slow down				

section 6

21 에디슨 그는 이미 전설이다.

22 모두를 벌벌 떨게 만드는 시카고 폭주족의 위협

23 세상에 진짜 공짜는 없다니, 훌쩍

24 물건은 만드는 게 아니고 파는 것이다.

inventor 〉〉 발명가

determination 〉〉 결단력

light bulb 〉〉 전구

learn 〉〉 배우다

tough 〉〉 거친

bar 〉〉 술집

stolen 〉〉 훔쳐진

order 〉〉 주문하다

a shot of whiskey 〉〉 위스키 한 잔

shout 〉〉 외치다

by the time 〉〉 ~할 때까지

happen 〉〉 일어나다

as well 〉〉 ~도 또한

as soon as 〉〉 ~하자마자

report 〉〉 보고하다

bartender 〉〉 바텐더

casually 〉〉 무심코

on foot 〉〉 걸어서

wish 〉〉 바라다

anonymously 〉〉 익명으로

fabulous 〉〉 끝내주는

mailbox 〉〉 우편함

perfume 〉〉 향수

hit the market 〉〉 출시하다

market 〉〉 시장

be able to 〉〉 ~할 수 있다

prestigious 〉〉 명성이 높은

cosmetic 〉〉 화장품

exhibit 〉〉 전시회, 시연회

spill 〉〉 엎지르다

crowd 〉〉 군중

scent 〉〉 냄새

21

에디슨,
그는 이미
전설이었다

Words

- inventor
- determination
- light bulb
- learn

Thomas Edison was not only a great inventor. He was also a man of strong determination. If he decided to do something, he did do it. That is how he invented the light bulb. Once, someone asked him, “I heard you tried to make the light bulb over a thousand times but always failed. How did it feel to fail so many times?” Edison replied, “I learned over a thousand wrong ways to build the light bulb. I didn’t fail at all.”

단어 추론

1 본문에서 색칠한 단어의 뜻을 문맥을 통해 추론해보세요.

	* 결단력
determination *	* 실패하다
invent *	* 발명하다
fail *	* 의구심
	* 노력하다

2 본문의 'Thomas Edison'에 관한 설명으로 옳지 않은 것은?

① He was a great inventor.

② He was a man who put his plan into action.

③ He invented the light bulb.

④ A light bulb was invented after more than a thousand tries.

⑤ He was a man who sometimes gave up easily.

22

모두를 벌벌 떨게 만드는 시카고 폭주족의 위엄

A tough biker left a bar after he found out that his bike was stolen. Being angry, he came back to the bar and ordered a shot of whiskey. He shouted, “If my bike is not back by the time I finish this whiskey, what happened in Chicago yesterday will happen here as well!” Many people left the bar in fear and began to search for his bike.

As soon as the biker stood up to leave, a man came into the bar and reported, “Your bike is back!” When the biker was about to leave the bar, the bartender asked what happened in Chicago. He replied casually, “I went back to my hotel on foot.”

Words

- tough
- left
- bar
- stolen
- order
- a shot of whiskey
- shout
- by the time
- happen
- as well
- as soon as
- report
- bartender
- casually
- on foot

단어 추론

1 본문에서 색칠한 단어의 뜻을 문맥을 통해 추론해보세요.

		*	소리치다
order	*	*	주문하다
casually	*	*	무심코
on foot	*	*	화나서
		*	걸어서

2 본문에 나온 폭주족이 그의 오토바이를 찾지 못했다면 어떤 일이 일어났을지 한글로 쓰세요.

정답 및 해설 p.16

23

세상에 진짜

공짜는 없다니

Words

wish
anonymously
fabulous
mailbox

James had a wish. He wanted to go to the movies. However, he had no money. He was very sad.

One day, he got a welcome surprise. Someone had sent him a ticket (a)anonymously! He asked everyone he knew if they had sent it, but they told him they had not. James went to the movies anyway. He had a (b)fabulous time.

When he came home, he found a letter in his mailbox. He opened it. It said, "Did you like the movie? Good! By the way, since you owe me money for the ticket, I'm taking your computer! Nothing is free, right?

1 다음 힌트가 되는 문장을 참고하여 밑줄 친 단어 (a)의 뜻을 문맥을 통해 추론해보세요.

> If you write a letter "anonymously", it means that you don't write about who you are.

2 다음 밑줄 친 단어 (b)와 문맥상 바꿔 쓸 수 있는 단어를 고르세요.

① disappointing ② sad ③ great
④ funny ⑤ annoying

3 본문에서 James는 우편함에 있는 편지를 읽었을 때 심경이 어땠을지 추론해보세요.

① grateful ② happy ③ tired
④ shocked ⑤ satisfied

정답 및 해설 p.17

24

In 1953, Estee Lauder's first perfume, "Youth Dew", hit the market. Even though it sold well in London, she was not able to get the prestigious stores in Paris to sell it.

During an important cosmetics exhibit in Paris, hiding her intention, Estee (a)"on purpose" spilled a bottle of her Youth Dew in the middle of a crowd. The scent spread quickly and many customers became interested in her products.

People could also try her perfumes at stores without buying them. Thanks to her smart marketing skills, Estee Lauder was able to build a successful cosmetics company.

물건은
만드는게 아니고
파는 것이다

Words

- perfume
- hit the market
- be able to
- prestigious
- exhibit
- intention
- spill
- crowd
- scent
- spread

단어 추론

1 본문에서 색칠한 단어의 뜻을 문맥을 통해 추론해보세요.

		*	전시하다
hit the market	*	*	고객
spill	*	*	엎지르다
scent	*	*	냄새
		*	출시하다

2 본문에서 밑줄 친 단어 (a)의 뜻을 문맥을 통해 추론해보세요.

---

3 위 글의 주제로 알맞은 것을 고르시오.

① 향수 'Youth Dew'의 제조 과정
② 에스티 로더의 마케팅 전략
③ 에스티 로더의 실수
④ 에스티 로더의 실패 이유
⑤ 향수 'Youth Dew'의 매력

4 본문에 언급된 Estee Lauder의 향수에 관한 설명과 일치하지 않는 것을 고르시오.

① Estee Lauder의 첫 향수는 1953년 출시되었다.
② 첫 향수는 영국에서 잘 팔렸다.
③ 출시하자마자 파리의 명품관에 입점했다.
④ 손님들은 매장에서 사지 않아도 뿌려볼 수 있었다.
⑤ Estee는 그녀의 향수를 화장품 시연회에서 엎지른 적이 있다.

section 6

Words Test

다음 영어 단어의 뜻을 적으시오.

01	inventor		18	casually	
02	determination		19	on foot	
03	light bulb		20	wish	
04	learn		21	anonymously	
05	tough		22	fabulous	
06	left		23	mailbox	
07	bar		24	perfume	
08	stolen		25	hit the market	
09	order		26	be able to	
10	a shot of whiskey		27	prestigious	
11	shout		28	exhibit	
12	by the time		29	intiontion	
13	happen		30	spill	
14	as well		31	crowd	
15	as soon as		32	scent	
16	report		33	spread	
17	bartender				

section 7

faithful 〉〉 충실한
slept 〉〉 sleep의 과거 (자다)
whenever 〉〉 ~할 때는 언제든지
woke up 〉〉 wake up의 과거 (깨다)
lick 〉〉 핥다
murder 〉〉 살인
neighborhood 〉〉 동네
reassured 〉〉 안심한
astronaut 〉〉 우주비행사
protection 〉〉 보호
space suit 〉〉 우주복
gravity 〉〉 중력
not ~ at all 〉〉 전혀 ~하지 않는
straw 〉〉 빨대
attached 〉〉 부착된
feature 〉〉 특징
miniature 〉〉 미니어처, 소형
spaceship 〉〉 우주선
diaper 〉〉 기저귀
celebrate 〉〉 축하하다
decide 〉〉 결정하다
invite 〉〉 초대하다
fairy 〉〉 요정
appear 〉〉 나타나다
faithfully 〉〉 성실하게
grant a wish 〉〉 소원을 들어주다
twirl 〉〉 휘두르다
wand 〉〉 요술지팡이
camping 〉〉 야영
hiking 〉〉 하이킹
discover 〉〉 발견하다
climb up 〉〉 올라가다
cliff 〉〉 절벽
laugh 〉〉 웃다
emerge 〉〉 나타나다
eventually 〉〉 결국에
sorrow 〉〉 슬픔
exactly 〉〉 정확히
quickly 〉〉 빨리
arrive 〉〉 도착하다
astonished 〉〉 깜짝 놀란
bow 〉〉 머리를 숙이다
track 〉〉 흔적
in front of 〉〉 ~의 앞에
tombstone 〉〉 묘비

25

주인님

저 여기 있어요

죄송...

Words

faithful
slept
whenever
woke up
lick
murder
neighborhood
reassured

Reese lived alone with her faithful dog, Spot. Spot always slept on the floor right next to Reese's bed. That way, whenever Reese woke up in the middle of the night, she could drop her hand on the side of the bed and Spot would always be there. He would lick her hand to let her know she was safe, and then, Reese would go back to sleep.

One night, Reese had trouble sleeping. She felt a little scared, because she had read an article in the newspaper about a murder that had happened in her neighborhood the day before. She dropped her hand on the side where Spot slept. As he always did, Spot licked her hand. Feeling (a)<u>reassured</u>, Reese began to get sleepy.

Just before she fell asleep, she looked out at the living room. To her surprise, she saw Spot standing there, looking at her. But if Spot had been in the living room all this time, then what had licked her hand only moments before?

단어 추론

1 본문에서 색칠한 단어의 뜻을 문맥을 통해 추론해보세요.

		*	무서운
faithful	*	*	살인
lick	*	*	충실한
murder	*	*	떨어뜨리다
		*	핥다

2 본문에서 밑줄 친 단어 (a)의 뜻을 문맥을 통해 추론해보세요.

____

3 다음 문장은 본문의 내용입니다. 빈칸에 알맞은 단어를 본문에서 찾아 쓰세요.

The next night when a murder happened in her neighborhood, something other than Spot ______________ ed her hand.

4 다음 중 본문 글의 종류를 고르세요.

① science ② romance ③ horror

④ comic ⑤ action

26

우주복에 대한

자세한 설명

What do astronauts wear in space? They wear space suits. Space suits serve as clothing and protection for astronauts. People consider the space suit to be very heavy to wear, since it weighs around 100kg. However, because there is no gravity in space, it is actually not heavy for the astronaut at all.

The space suit has many features. Astronauts can eat and drink through a straw attached to a food supply on the suit. And if they need to use the bathroom, they just do it without taking off their suit, because they were always wearing a (a)diaper. In a way, it is almost like a miniature spaceship.

Words

- astronaut
- protection
- space suit
- gravity
- not ~ at all
- straw
- attached
- feature
- miniature
- spaceship
- diaper

단어 추론

1 본문에서 색칠한 단어의 뜻을 문맥을 통해 추론해보세요.

		*	특징
astronaut	*	*	중력
gravity	*	*	우주선
feature	*	*	우주
		*	우주비행사

2 본문에 대한 설명과 일치하지 않는 것을 고르세요.

① 우주복은 우주비행사들의 옷과 보호의 기능을 한다.

② 사람들은 우주복을 입으면 매우 무거울 것이라 생각한다.

③ 우주비행사들은 우주복이 무겁다고 전혀 생각하지 않는다.

④ 우주비행사들은 용변을 볼 때 우주복을 벗어야 한다.

⑤ 우주비행사들은 우주복과 연결된 빨대로 음식을 섭취한다.

3 본문에서 밑줄 친 단어 (a)의 뜻을 문맥을 통해 추론해보세요.

____

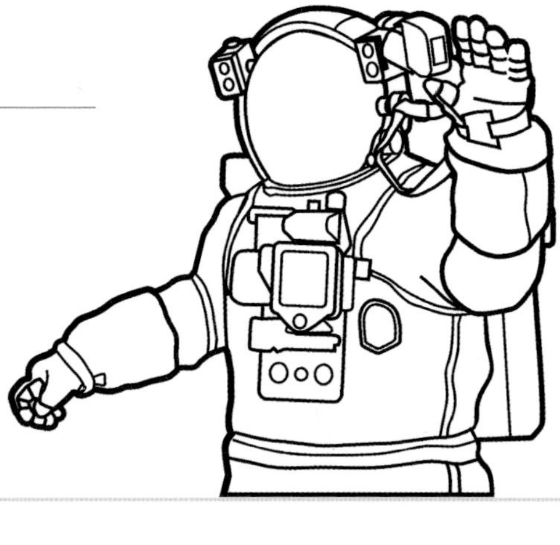

정답 및 해설 p.19

27

할아버지의

속마음

It was a man's 60th birthday. To celebrate, he and his wife decided to have a party. They invited friends and family and neighbors, but they never invited a fairy. ① So, you can imagine their surprise when a fairy appeared in their living room! The fairy told them that since they had been faithfully married for 25 years, she would grant each one a wish.

② The woman said, "We've never had any money to travel. My wish is to see the whole world!" The fairy twirled her wand, and two plane tickets appeared in the woman's hand!

③ The man thought for a while. Then, he cautiously said, "I wish I could be married to a woman who is 30 years younger than I am!" ④ The fairy twirled her wand, and his wish was also granted. ⑤ On his 60th birthday, he became 90 years old.

Words

- celebrate
- decide
- invite
- fairy
- appear
- faithfully
- grant a wish
- twirl
- wand

단어 추론

1 본문에서 색칠한 단어의 뜻을 문맥을 통해 추론해보세요.

		*	들어주다
faithfully	*	*	만족하여
grant	*	*	조심스럽게
cautiously	*	*	충실히
		*	당당하게

정답 및 해설 p.20

2 본문에 대한 설명과 일치하지 않는 것을 고르세요.

① 부부는 남편의 60번째 생일을 축하하기 위해 파티를 열었다.

② 부인은 남편 몰래 파티에 요정을 초대했다.

③ 요정은 부부의 소원을 하나씩 들어주었다.

④ 부인의 소원은 세계여행이었다.

⑤ 남편의 소원은 자신보다 30살 어린 여자와 결혼하는 것이었다.

3 본문에서 다음 문장이 들어가기에 가장 알맞은 곳은?

> The fairy then asked the woman' s husband what he wished for.

① ② ③ ④ ⑤

28

그들 중 누가
집에 갈 수
있었을까

Words

camping
hiking
discover
climb up
cliff
laugh
emerge
eventually
sorrow
exactly
quickly
arrive
astonished
bow
track
in front of
tombstone

One day, five friends went camping. They were hiking in the mountains when they discovered a small lake. Because they were very hot, they decided to go swimming in the lake. After swimming for a while, one of the friends climbed up the side of a cliff and jumped into the water. The four friends laughed and waited for him to emerge.

However, they became worried when their friend did not appear. They dived in and searched the water for their friend, but they did not find any trace of him. They eventually stopped and climbed out of the water. They were in great sorrow. The four friends made a promise to each other that they would return exactly one year later.

The year passed quickly. The four friends came back to the lake to remember their dead friend. However, when they arrived at the lake, they were (a)astonished. Their friend was in front of them! Their friend was standing with his back to them. His head was bowed. They became very excited and ran towards their friend. They soon saw
something that stopped them in their tracks. In front of their friend were four tombstones with their names on them.

단어 추론

1 본문에서 색칠한 단어의 뜻을 문맥을 통해 추론해보세요.

		*	발견하다
discover	*	*	뛰어들다
emerge	*	*	슬픔
sorrow	*	*	기쁨
		*	나타나다

2 다음 밑줄 친 단어 (a)와 문맥상 바꿔 쓸 수 있는 단어를 고르세요.

① tired

② moved

③ reassured

④ depressed

⑤ shocked

3 본문에 밑줄 친 문장이 의미하는 것을 한글로 쓰세요.

section 7

Words Test

다음 영어 단어의 뜻을 적으시오.

01	faithful		23	fairy	
02	slept		24	appear	
03	whenever		25	faithfully	
04	woke up		26	grant a wish	
05	lick		27	twirl	
06	murder		28	camping	
07	neighborhood		29	hiking	
08	reassured		30	discover	
09	astronaut		31	climb up	
10	protection		32	cliff	
11	space suit		33	laugh	
12	gravity		34	emerge	
13	not ~ at all		35	eventually	
14	straw		36	sorrow	
15	attached		37	exactly	
16	feature		38	quickly	
17	miniature		39	arrive	
18	spaceship		40	astonished	
19	diaper		41	bow	
20	celebrate		42	track	
21	decide		43	In front of	
22	invite		44	tombstone	

section 8

29 효도 아닌 효도

30 길냥이들에게 잘해줍시다.

31 두뇌 풀가동하고 수수께끼 시작!

32 부자라 아내가 예쁜 걸가,
아내가 예뻐서 부자가 된 걸까?

elementary school 〉〉 초등학교
named 〉〉 이름을 가진
raise 〉〉 들다
excellent 〉〉 훌륭한
visit 〉〉 방문하다
role 〉〉 역할
ancient 〉〉 고대의
Egyptian 〉〉 이집트인
society 〉〉 사회
once 〉〉 한때
wild cat 〉〉 야생 고양이
grain 〉〉 곡식
mice 〉〉 mouse의 복수 (쥐)
close 〉〉 가까운
consider 〉〉 여기다
in fact 〉〉 사실
prohibit 〉〉 금지하다
harm 〉〉 해치다
sentence 〉〉 선고하다
eyebrow 〉〉 눈썹
grief 〉〉 슬픔
sign 〉〉 표시
mourn 〉〉 애도하다
shot 〉〉 쏘다, 찍다
dip 〉〉 담그다
hung up 〉〉 hang up의 과거 (걸다)
take a picture 〉〉 사진을 찍다
flesh 〉〉 살
feather 〉〉 깃털
scale 〉〉 비늘
trip over 〉〉 전복되다
wet 〉〉 젖은
go up 〉〉 오르다
come down 〉〉 내리다
butter 〉〉 버터
outline 〉〉 윤곽
held 〉〉 hold의 과거분사 (담다)
sauce 〉〉 소스
president 〉〉 사장
wear 〉〉 입다
nightgown 〉〉 나이트 가운
unique 〉〉 독특한
success 〉〉 성공

29

효도 아닌

효도

Words

elementary school
named
raise
excellent
visit

An elementary school teacher was teaching her young students about making people feel glad. She asked her students if they had made someone feel glad. A young boy named Andrew raised his hand. "I made my grandmother glad yesterday," he said. "Excellent! How did you do it?" The teacher asked.

He told her, "I visited my grandmother yesterday for four hours. After four hours, I told her I was going to go home. She said, 'I'm glad you are.'"

단어 추론

1 본문에서 색칠한 단어의 뜻을 문맥을 통해 추론해보세요.

		*	화난
glad	*	*	방문하다
excellent	*	*	심각한
visit	*	*	훌륭한
		*	기쁜

2 본문에서 할머니가 밑줄 친 문장처럼 말한 이유는 무엇인지 한글로 쓰세요.

____

정답 및 해설 p.22

30

길냥이들에게
잘해줍시다

Cats played a very important role in ancient Egyptian society. Once, because wild cats were excellent hunters, they could protect Egyptian stores of grain from hungry mice. So, Egyptians and cats came very close. Egyptians considered cats so important, in fact, that laws prohibited the harming and killing of cats! People could be sentenced to death for killing a cat. When cats died, they even had funerals. People would shave their eyebrows, which was a sign of grief, and mourn the death of their cat.

Words

role
ancient
Egyptian
society
once
wild cat
grain
mice
close
consider
in fact
prohibit
harm
sentence
eyebrow
grief
sign
mourn

단어 추론

1 본문에서 색칠한 단어의 뜻을 문맥을 통해 추론해보세요.

		*	금지하다
role	*	*	사냥꾼
prohibit	*	*	역할
mourn	*	*	애도하다
		*	장례식

2 다음 본문에 관련된 질문에 한글로 대답하세요.

(1) 고대 이집트 사람들은 언제 눈썹을 밀었나요?

____

(2) 고대 이집트 사람들은 왜 눈썹을 밀었나요?

____

3 본문을 읽고 추론할 수 <u>없는</u> 것은 무엇인가요?

① 고대 이집트 사람들은 고양이와 매우 가까웠다.

② 고대 이집트 사람들은 고양이를 중시했다.

③ 고대 이집트 사회에서는 고양이를 죽이면 처벌했다.

④ 고대 이집트 사람들은 고양이와 개를 함께 키웠다.

⑤ 고대 이집트 사회에서는 고양이도 죽으면 장례식을 해줬다.

정답 및 해설 p.22

31

Questions

두뇌 풀가동하고
수수께끼 시작!

Words

shot
dip
hung up
take a picture
flesh
feather
scale
trip over
wet
go up
come down
butter
harm
sentence
eyebrow

1. A man shot his wife, dipped underwater, hung up, and the next day morning they had a nice breakfast. How?

2. I have no flesh, feathers, scales, or bones. But, I have fingers. Who am I?

3. There were four men on a boat. The boat tripped over and not a single men got wet. How?

4. What two things can you never eat for breakfast?

5. What goes up and never comes down?

6. Why did the boy throw the butter out of his window?

Answers

1. The man took a picture of his wife.
   (He dunked the picture underwater, and hung it up to dry it.)

2. Gloves

3. They were all married

4. Lunch and dinner.

5. Your age

6. He wanted to see a butter fly.

32

부자라서
아내가 예쁜걸까,
아내가 예뻐서
부자가 된 걸까?

Words

outline
held
sauce
president
wear
nightgown
unique
success

What do you think the Coca-Cola bottle looks like? Do outlines of the bottle make you think of anything? Long time ago, when Coca-Cola was first sold, it was put into bottles that held sauces for cooking. Not long after, the president of Coca-Cola thought that the bottle needed to be unique. He thought long and hard about the design of the new bottle, but he could not think of anything. One evening, he was at home still thinking about the bottle when he saw his wife wearing her nightgown. The outline of her figure was very beautiful. As soon as he saw her, the president knew what the bottle should look like. His bottle was a great success.

단어 추론

1 본문에서 색칠한 단어의 뜻을 문맥을 통해 추론해보세요.

		*	윤곽
outline	*	*	평범한
unique	*	*	성공
success	*	*	실패
		*	독특한

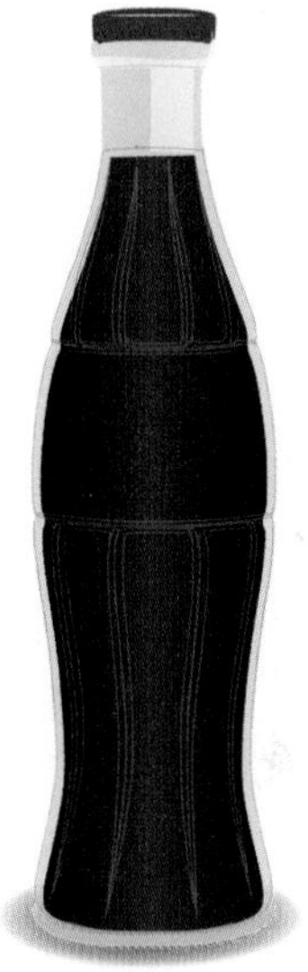

2 다음 중 본문의 제목으로 적절한 것을 고르세요.

① 새로운 소스를 만드는 방법

② 콜라 병 모양의 유래

③ 코카 콜라 사장 부인의 아이디어

④ 코카 콜라의 연간 매출 수익

⑤ 코카 콜라 판매 전략

3 현재 우리가 사먹는 콜라 병의 모양을 어디에서 아이디어를 얻었는지 한글로 쓰세요.

정답 및 해설 p.24

Words Test

다음 영어 단어의 뜻을 적으시오.

01	elementary school		23	mourn	
02	named		24	shot	
03	raise		25	dip	
04	excellent		26	hung up	
05	visit		27	take a picture	
06	role		28	flesh	
07	ancient		29	feather	
08	Egyptian		30	scale	
09	society		31	trip over	
10	once		32	wet	
11	wild cat		33	go up	
12	grain		34	come down	
13	mice		35	butter	
14	close		36	outline	
15	consider		37	held	
16	in fact		38	sauce	
17	prohibit		39	president	
18	harm		40	wear	
19	sentence		41	nightgown	
20	eyebrow		42	unique	
21	grief		43	success	
22	sign				

section 9

seem 〉〉 ~로 보이다
cheaper 〉〉 더 싼
expect 〉〉 기대하다
deal 〉〉 거래
department store 〉〉 백화점
rest room 〉〉 화장실
usually 〉〉 보통
several 〉〉 여러 개의
product 〉〉 제품
display 〉〉 진열
prevent 〉〉 방해하다
hurry 〉〉 재촉하다
wives 〉〉 wife의 복수 (아내)
comfortable 〉〉 편안한
likewise 〉〉 마찬가지로
grocery store 〉〉 식료품점
checkout counter 〉〉 계산대
moreover 〉〉 더욱이
historical 〉〉 역사적인
question 〉〉 질문
ancient 〉〉 고대의
ingredient 〉〉 성분
toothpaste 〉〉 치약
urine 〉〉 오줌
Portuguese 〉〉 포르투갈인
effective 〉〉 효과적인
whiten 〉〉 희게 하다
close to 〉〉 ~에 가까이
understand 〉〉 이해하다
German 〉〉 독일어
murder 〉〉 살해하다
coincidence 〉〉 우연의 일치
Alaska 〉〉 알래스카
far from 〉〉 ~로부터 먼
large 〉〉 큰
one-fifth 〉〉 5분의 1
covered by 〉〉 ~로 뒤덮힌
glacier 〉〉 빙하
including 〉〉 ~을 포함하여
environment 〉〉 환경
explorer 〉〉 탐험가
trader 〉〉 상인
sea otter 〉〉 해달
built 〉〉 build의 과거분사 (짓다)
therefor 〉〉 그러므로
million 〉〉 100만
huge 〉〉 거대한
cost 〉〉 비용
per 〉〉 ~당
acre 〉〉 에이커 (면적의 단위)
In spite of 〉〉 ~에도 불구하고
amazingly 〉〉 놀랍게도
purchase 〉〉 사다, 구매하다
resource 〉〉 자원
salmon 〉〉 연어
lumber 〉〉 목재
rich 〉〉 풍요로운

33

괘씸하기도
하지만
꽤 재미있는
마케팅 전략

When you go shopping, you can easily see numbers like 9,900 or 19,900. It is because they seem much cheaper than 10,000 or 20,000. In this way, people buy things more than they expect, because they feel they are getting a good deal.

In department stores, rest rooms are usually in long away corners of each floor and they are not even on the first floor. You have to walk out of your way to get there. By doing this, you have a chance to look at several products and displays.

Department stores even don't have any clock and windows so that you can forget about the time and stay longer. Moreover, to prevent husbands from hurrying their wives, there are always comfortable chairs in department stores. Likewise, in supermarkets or grocery stores, there are chocolates and candy bars at the checkout counter. Why? Because people can buy them when they pay for other things.

Words

- seem
- cheaper
- expect
- deal
- department store
- rest room
- usually
- several
- product
- display
- prevent
- hurry
- wives
- comfortable
- likewise
- grocery store
- checkout counter
- moreover

단어 추론

1 본문에서 색칠한 단어의 뜻을 문맥을 통해 추론해보세요.

		*	편안한
cheap	*	*	가격이 싼
comfortable	*	*	재촉하다
checkout counter	*	*	계산대
		*	보관함

2 다음 중 본문에서 언급한 마케팅 전략과 다른 것은?

① 백화점은 편안한 의자들을 비치해 놓는다.

② 백화점에는 시계와 창문이 없다.

③ 백화점 1층에는 화장실이 없다.

④ 식료품점에는 화장실이 구석에 있다.

⑤ 식료품점에는 계산대에 초콜릿이나 사탕을 둔다.

3 이 밖에도 알고 있거나 예상이 되는 가게의 마케팅 전략을 자유롭게 한글로 쓰세요.

34

Let me ask you three historical questions!

세 가지
흥미로운
역사적 사실들

Words

historical
question
ancient
ingredient
toothpaste
urine
Prtuguese
effective
whiten
close to
understand
German
murder
coincidence

1. **What did ancient Romans use as an ingredient in their toothpaste?**
It was human urine. Even some rich Romans bought Portuguese men's urine and used it, because they thought that it was more effective to whiten teeth.

2. **When Albert Einstein died, what were his last words?**
Nobody knows what his last words were, because he said something but the nurse close to him did not understand German.

3. **In 1911, Sir Edmund Godfrey at Greenberry Hill was murdered by three men. What were their names?**
Their names were Green, Berry and Hill.
What a (a)coincidence!

단어 추론

1 본문에서 색칠한 단어의 뜻을 문맥을 통해 추론해보세요.

		* 효과적인
ingredient	*	* 이해하다
effective	*	* 약품
murder	*	* 재료
		* 살해하다

2 본문에서 밑줄 친 단어(a)의 뜻을 문맥을 통해 추론해보세요.

3 본문을 읽고 추론할 수 없는 것은 무엇인가요?

① 오줌이 치약의 재료로 쓰였던 적이 있었다.

② 로마사람들은 이를 하얗게 하려는 노력을 하곤 했다.

③ 아인슈타인은 임종 직전 독일어로 말을 남겼다.

④ 아인슈타인 옆에 있던 간호사는 독일인이 아니었다.

⑤ 애드먼드경을 살해한 범인들의 이름은 모두 같았다.

35

황금알을 품은

알레스카

Words

Alaska
far from
large
one-fifth
covered by
glacier
including
environment
explorer
trader
sea otter
built
therefore
million
huge
cost
per
acre
in spite of
amazingly
purchase
resource
salmon
lumber
rich

Alaska is one of the states of America, but it is very far from most American lands. Alaska is the largest state in the United States, as it consists of one-fifth of the entire country. The state is covered by very big glaciers and snow-topped mountains, including Mt. McKinley, the highest mountain in North America. A lot of tourists travel to Alaska each year to hike, hunt and fish in its beautiful environment.

Russian explorers discovered Alaska in 1741, and Russian fur traders soon started hunting in the sea around Alaska for sea otters. They also built castles and towns. However, in the end, Russia decided that Alaska was too far away for Russians to live in. Therefore, Russia sold Alaska to the United States in 1867 for $7.2 million. The huge state cost only 2 cents per acre.

*sea otter 해달

In spite of its amazingly cheap price, many Americans considered the purchase as a big mistake. Newspapers nicknamed the new area "Seward's Icebox" after the Secretary of State, William Henry Seward, who purchased it.

However, later discoveries proved Alaska to be a great resource. In 1896, gold was discovered in the state, so thousands moved to Alaska to get rich. The state is also a rich source of salmon, lumber, and oil as well as an amazing place for tourists to visit. The state once called "Seward's Icebox" is currently one of America's richest and most beautiful places.

단어 추론

1 본문에서 색칠한 단어의 뜻을 문맥을 통해 추론해보세요.

		*	빙하
glacier	*	*	발견하다
purchase	*	*	현재
currently	*	*	목재
		*	구매하다

정답 및 해설 p.26

2 알래스카가 한 때 "Seward' s Icebox"란 별명을 가졌던 이유를 한글로 쓰세요.

3 본문에 나온 알래스카에 대한 설명과 일치하지 않는 것을 고르세요.

① 미국 전체 주들의 5분의 1크기이다.

② 미국이 사기 전에는 러시아의 영토였다.

③ 구입을 결정한 것은 William Henry Seward였다.

④ 러시아가 팔기로 결정한 이유는 너무 척박한 땅이기 때문이다.

⑤ 구입 후 여론이 긍정적이지는 않았다

section 9

Words Test

다음 영어 단어의 뜻을 적으시오.

01	seem		30	German	
02	cheaper		31	murder	
03	expect		32	coincidence	
04	deal		33	Alaska	
05	department store		34	far from	
06	rest room		35	large	
07	usually		36	one-fifth	
08	several		37	covered by	
09	product		38	glacier	
10	display		39	including	
11	prevent		40	environment	
12	hurry		41	explorer	
13	wives		42	trader	
14	comfortable		43	sea otter	
15	likewise		44	built	
16	grocery store		45	therefore	
17	checkout counter		46	million	
18	moreover		47	huge	
19	historical		48	cost	
20	question		49	per	
21	ancient		50	acre	
22	ingredient		51	In spite of	
23	toothpaste		52	amazingly	
24	urine		53	purchase	
25	Portuguese		54	resource	
26	effective		55	salmon	
27	whiten		56	lumber	
28	close to		57	rich	
29	understand				

section 10

wave 〉〉 손을 흔들다

none 〉〉 아무도 ~ 않다

discouraged 〉〉 낙담한

shabby 〉〉 초라한

introduce 〉〉 소개하다

owe 〉〉 빚지다

pay forward 〉〉 선행을 베풀다

drove off 〉〉 drive off의 과거 (떠나다)

revenge 〉〉 복수

mean 〉〉 의미하다

stage 〉〉 단계

lock 〉〉 잠그다

allow 〉〉 허락하다

awful 〉〉 끔찍한

frustrated 〉〉 좌절한

endure 〉〉 견디다

hardship 〉〉 어려움

36

세상은 아직
살만한가봅니다

Words

- wave
- none
- discouraged
- shabby
- introduce
- owe
- pay forward
- drove off

An old woman was standing on the side of the road. She was standing there, because her car had a flat tire. She waved at passing cars, but none stopped. The woman became discouraged and stopped waving.

But, suddenly, a car stopped next to her. Because the driver looked shabby, she got a little worried. He introduced himself as James Ryan and he quickly changed the flat tire on the woman's car. When he was about to go back to his car, the woman grabbed his arm. "How much do I owe you for helping me?" she asked.

The man just smiled kindly. "If you really feel like you owe me, then pay it forward. When you see someone who needs help, think of me and help that person." Saying that, the man went back to his car and drove off.

중간점검

잘 이해하고 있나요?

단어 추론

1 본문에서 색칠한 단어의 뜻을 문맥을 통해 추론해보세요.

		*	기분 좋은
discouraged	*	*	남루한
shabby	*	*	낙담한
pay forward	*	*	빚을 갚다
		*	선행을 베풀다

2 남자는 할머니를 도와드린 대가로 무엇을 원했는지 한글로 쓰세요.

정답 및 해설 p.27

That evening, the woman went to a small restaurant. The restaurant looked dirty and there were few customers. The only waitress was a very pregnant, tired young woman. However, she was very kind and welcomed the old woman warmly. The old woman decided to help the young woman. She asked the waitress to get her some more water.

When the waitress returned, the old woman had disappeared. On the table were five hundred dollars and a note, which said: “(a)Someone was kind to me and helped me today. I want to pay it forward. If you can, please help someone in need, too”.

When the young waitress got home, her husband was already sleeping. Sitting next to her sleeping husband, she quietly told him about the old woman and her note. How could she know we really need money for the baby who will soon arrive? She smiled and whispered to her snoring husband, "Everything's going to be ok. Everything's going to be ok. I love you, James Ryan."

잘 이해하고 있나요?

1 할머니가 밑줄 친 문장처럼 행동한 이유를 자유롭게 한글로 쓰세요.

2 밑줄 친 (a)someone과 여종업원과의 관계가 어떻게 되나요?

① 남남

② 남매

③ 부부

❀ 종합문제 ❀

1 다음 중 본문 글은 어떤 종류의 이야기인지 고르세요.

① touching

② romantic

③ horror

④ humorous

⑤ amusing

2 본문과 가장 관련이 깊은 속담을 골라보세요.

① 등잔 밑이 어둡다.

② 뿌린 대로 거둔다.

③ 뚝배기보다는 장맛이다.

④ 친구 따라 강남 간다.

⑤ 될성부른 나무는 떡잎부터 알아본다.

3 본문에 대한 설명과 일치하지 않는 것을 고르세요.

① 할머니 차의 타이어가 펑크가 났다.

② 할머니를 도와준 남자는 남루해 보였다.

③ 할머니를 도와준 남자는 할머니로부터 돈을 받았다.

④ 레스토랑 여종업원은 만삭이었다.

⑤ 레스토랑 여종업원은 매우 친절했다.

정답 및 해설 p.28

37

판도라의 상자

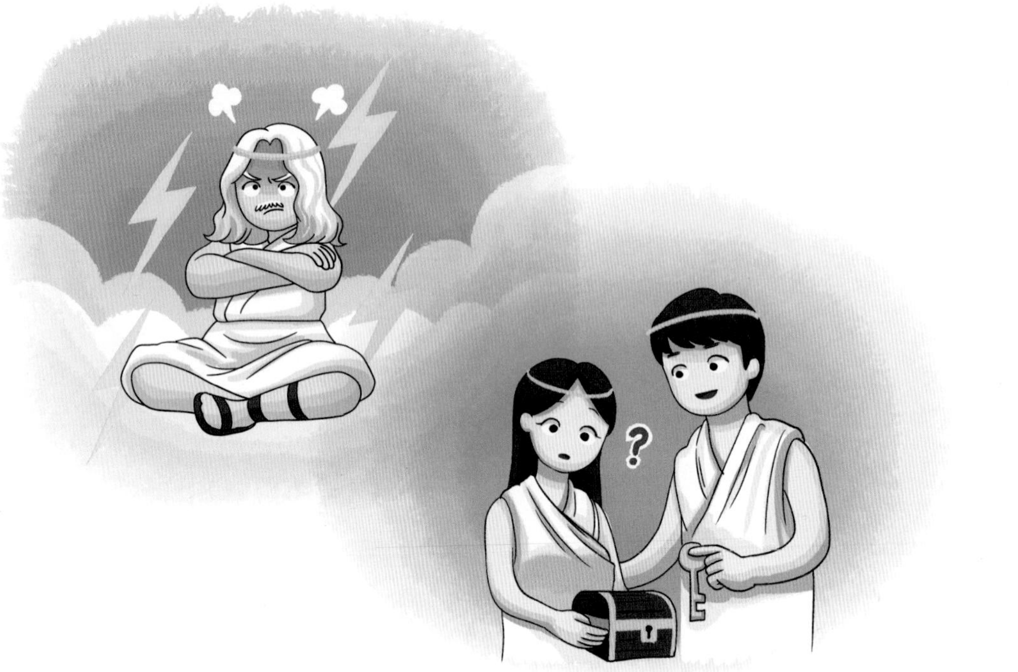

Words

- revenge
- mean
- stage
- lock
- allow
- awful
- frustrated
- endure
- hardship

Zeus decided to get revenge. Prometheus made Zeus very angry, because he stole fire from gods and gave it to men. So, Zeus ordered Hephaistos to create a beautiful and lovely woman, and he named her Pandora, which means "all-gifts".

Zeus began the next stage of his plan. He introduced Prometheus' brother, Epimetheus to Pandora, and let them get married. Then, Zeus gave Pandora a small box that was locked. He gave Epimetheus the key to the box, and told him never to open it.

Pandora wanted very much to open the box and find out what was inside. However, Epimetheus would never allow her to open it. One day, while Epimetheus was sleeping, she saw her chance. She took the key and unlocked the box.

중간점검

잘 이해하고 있나요?

1 **프로메테우스가 제우스를 화나게 한 이유를 한글로 쓰세요.**

2 **본문에 나온 "판도라"에 대해 추론할 수 없는 것은?**

① 미모가 빼어나다.

② 호기심이 많다.

③ 부모가 인간이다.

정답 및 해설 p.29

As soon as Pandora opened the box, terrible things burst out. Hate, jealousy, crimes, worry, illness, and many more awful things that had never existed before flew into the sky and disappeared. Pandora tried her best to grab the flying evils and put them back. However, they were all out of her reach. How she regretted opening the box!

Pandora plopped down in front of the opened box and screamed and cried. (a)Frustrated, she saw the box again and there was something shining and beautiful on the box. The thing was Hope. Zeus had included Hope in the box, so that people could ⓐendure and overcome ⓑhardships in life.

잘 이해하고 있나요?

1 다음 밑줄 친 (a)의 의미를 문맥을 통해 추론하세요.

① 신이 난

② 좌절한

③ 감동한

2 다음 ⓐ, ⓑ의 단어 뜻으로 적절히 연결된 것을 고르세요.

	ⓐ		ⓑ
①	연마하고 단련하다	-	지혜들을
②	견디고 극복하다	-	고난들
③	놓치지 말고 붙잡다	-	기회들

정답 및 해설 p.29

❀ 종합문제 ❀

1 본문에 대한 설명과 일치하지 않는 것을 고르세요.

① 프로메테우스는 판도라와 결혼했다.

② 프로메테우스는 제우스를 화나게 했다.

③ 제우스가 처음부터 판도라에게 열쇠를 준 것은 아니었다.

④ 판도라는 결국 남편의 말을 듣지 않았다.

⑤ 판도라는 상자를 연 것을 후회했다.

2 우리는 보통 언제 "판도라의 상자를 열었다." 라는 표현을 쓰나요?

① 뜻밖에 횡재가 있었을 때

② 남의 비밀을 지키지 않았을 때

③ 과하게 지출을 했을 때

④ 하지 말았어야 하는 일을 했을 때

⑤ 주변 사람의 지갑에 손을 댔을 때

Words Test

다음 영어 단어의 뜻을 적으시오.

01	wave		10	mean	
02	none		11	stage	
03	discouraged		12	lock	
04	shabby		13	allow	
05	introduce		14	awful	
06	owe		15	frustrated	
07	pay forward		16	endure	
08	drove off		17	hardship	
09	revenge				

핵꿀잼 Reading

LEVEL 1

| 정답 및 해설 |

section 1

01 / 쟤가 제니? 본문 p.10

grocery	식료품
aisle	코너, 통로
ask	요구하다
began	begin의 과거 (시작하다)
scream	소리치다
plop down	철푸덕 앉다
refuse	거절하다
continue	지속하다
stood	stand의 과거 (서다)
daughter	딸
murmur	중얼거리다
worry	걱정하다
calm	침착한
nearby	근처에
gentle	상냥한

정답

1. grocery - 식료품
   plop down - 털썩 주저앉다
   murmur - 중얼거리다

2. ①　　3. ④

2. ①
   ①번만 딸을 가리키고, 나머지는 다 엄마를 가리킨다.

3. ④
   엄마가 딸을 달래준 것이 아니고 자기 자신을 진정시키는 것이었는데 지나가는 사람은 딸을 달랜다고 생각했다.

해석

한 젊은 엄마가 그녀의 딸과 장을 보고 있었다. 그들이 사탕 코너를 지나갈 때, 그 어린 소녀는 엄마한테 사탕을 요구했다. 엄마가 안된다고 하자, 소녀는 소리지르고 울기 시작했다. 아이는 땅에 주저앉아서 움직이길 거부했다. 그녀는 계속해서 소리지르고 울었다.

엄마는 딸 옆에 서서, 중얼거리기 시작했다. "괜찮아 제니야, 괜찮아. 걱정하지마. 소리지르지 말렴. 진정해. 다 잘 될 거야, 제니야." 근처에 있던 나이든 아줌마가 그녀에게 제니한테 어떻게 이런 상냥한 엄마가 다 있을 수 있냐고 말했다. 그러자 엄마는 아줌마에게 말했다. "제가 제니인데요."

02 / 진짜 아프다면 머리 굴리지 마세요. 본문 p.12

catch a cold	감기에 걸리다
while	~동안
answer	대답하다
however	그러나
charge	청구하다
hear	듣다
visit	방문하다
examine	검사하다
glad	기쁜
gave	give의 과거 (주다)
medicine	약
recover	회복하다

정답

1. charge - 부과하다
   examine - 검사하다
   medicine - 약

2. ④　　3. ⑤

2. ④

첫 방문보다 두 번째 진료비가 더 저렴하다는 것을 안 잭은 일부러 진료비를 적게 내려고 의사에게 다시 방문한 것처럼 가장했다.

3. ⑤

진료비를 적게 내려고 꼼수를 부린 잭이 뛰는 놈이라면 그 의도를 바로 간파하고 맞대응 한 의사는 나는 놈이라고 볼 수 있다.

해석

잭은 호텔에 머무르는 동안 감기에 걸렸다, 그래서 잭은 안내 데스크에 괜찮은 의사를 알고 있는지 물었다. 직원이 대답하길, "물론이죠! 저는 괜찮은 의사를 알아요. 그런데, 그분은 첫 방문에는 30달러를 받고요, 두 번째와 세 번째 방문에는 10달러를 받으세요."

이것을 들은, 잭은 미소를 지었다. 왜냐하면 좋은 생각이 났기 때문이다. 그는 의사를 방문해서 말했다. "안녕하세요 의사 선생님, 저 또 왔어요." 의사는 잭을 잠시 동안 검진하고 나서 잭에게 말했다. "잭, 제가 저번에 당신에게 좋은 약을 줬었기에 다행이네요. 그걸 계속 먹는 것이 좋겠어요. 금방 좋아질 거에요."

03 / 내 목걸이가 점점 무거워지는 이유는? 본문 p.14

Papua New Guinea	파푸아뉴기니
traditional	전통적인
native	원주민
necklace	목걸이
strange	이상한
scary	무서운
custom	관습

정답

1. traditional – 전통적인
   necklace – 목걸이
   strange – 이상한
2. fingers 3. 해설 참고

2. fingers

파푸아뉴기니 여자들은 손가락으로 만든 목걸이를 하고 있다.

3. 예시 답안

해석

파푸아뉴기니 사람들은 여전히 매우 전통적이다. 많은 파푸아뉴기니의 원주민 남자들은 일부 손가락이 없다. 그들의 전통에 의하면, 만약 두 젊은 남자들이 싸우게 되면, 승자가 패자의 손가락을 자른다. 그리고 그 손가락을 그의 여자친구나 아내에게 준다. 그러면 그녀는 그것을 가지고 목걸이를 만들어 목에 걸고 다닌다. 참 이상하고 무서운 관습이다.

04 / 그녀와 가까워질수록 점점 살이 찌는데

본문 p.16

thin	날씬한
expensive	비싼
delicious	맛있는
order	주문하다
overcome	극복하다
temptation	유혹
end up -ing	결국 ~하다
not at all	전혀, 결코~아닌
accidentally	우연히
heard	hear의 과거 (듣다)

정답

1. ③ **2.** ③ **3.** 나는 유혹을 이길 수 없다. **4.** ①, ③

1. ③ 비열한

본문에서 셀린이 남이 살찌는 것을 보면 행복하다고 하는 대목이 있다. 본인은 항상 다이어트를 하면서 남이 살찌는 것을 보기 위해 의도적으로 음식까지 주문해서 먹도록 하는 행동을 봤을 때, 비열하다고 볼 수 있다.

① 친근한 ② 정직한

④ 불친절한 ⑤ 사려 깊은

2. ③ 속상한, 화난

글 마지막 쪽을 보면 셀린을 차버리고 싶다는 표현까지 하는 것을 봐서는 이 글을 쓸 때도 분노가 남아 있음이 느껴진다.

① 행복한 ② 만족한

④ 슬픈 ⑤ 피곤한

3. 나는 유혹을 이길 수 없다

이 문장을 기준으로 앞쪽에는 셀린이 비싸고 맛있는 음식을 주문한다는 이야기가 나오고, 뒤쪽에는 결국 먹어버린다는 의미가 나온다.

* overcome 극복하다 | temptation 유혹

4. ①, ③

주인공과 Celine이 절친이라고는 하지만 동갑이라는 말은 없다. 배려하는 척하는 정도이지 셀린의 행동은 사실 본인의 즐거움을 위한 것이라는 것이 글 마지막 쯤에 드러난다.

해석

나의 가장 친한 친구인 셀린은 아름답다. 또한 그녀는 나이에 비해 날씬하고 키까지 크다. 하지만 그녀는 항상 살을 더 빼길 원한다. 그녀는 항상 건강해지고 날씬해지는 것에 대해서 이야기한다. 우리가 함께 레스토랑에 가면, 그녀는 비싸고 맛있는 음식을 선택한다. 그리고 그녀는 친절하게 말한다. "너를 위해서 주문했어, 먹어~난 너무 배불러." 그러면 나는 유혹을 이기지 못하고 결국 그녀의 음식을 먹고 만다.

당신은 그녀가 왜 나한테 이러는지 아는가? 당신이 생각하기엔 그녀가 너무 친절하고 착해서 그러는 것 같은가? 전혀!! 어느 날, 나는 우연히 셀린이 그녀의 친구에게 이야기하는 것을 들었다. 그녀는 말하길, "난 누군가가 살찌는 것을 보면 너무 행복해." 어떻게 이럴 수가 있지? 난 정말 그녀를 차버리고 싶어.

section 2

05 / 어쩌면 그는 소시오패스일지도 본문 p.20

look for	찾다
seat	자리
curious	궁금한
sit on	앉다
empty	비어있는
replied	reply의 과거 (응답하다)
funeral	장례식

정답

1. curious - 궁금한
   empty - 비어있는
   funeral - 장례식
2. his family members or relatives
3. ④ 4. ①

3. ④ 당황한

아내가 죽은 지 얼마 안돼서 모두들 장례식에 가있는 동안 아무렇지 않게 야구를 보러 오고, 아내 몫의 표를 다른 사람에게 넘기려고까지 했다는 것을 알았을 때 조의 심경은 보기 중에서는 "당황한" 이 가장 잘 어울릴 것이다.

① 슬픈 ② 동정적인, 공감되는
③ 감동받은 ⑤ 웃기는

4. ①

슬픔에 잠겼다는 내용은 본문 어디에도 없으며 추론할 수도 없다.

해석

조는 야구 경기장에 있었다. 그가 자리를 찾고 있을 때, 한 남자가 한 좌석에 앉아 있고, 다른 좌석에는 가방과 코트를 올려둔 것을 봤다. 조는 궁금해졌다. 그는 그 남자에게 왜 티켓을 두 장이나 샀냐고 물었다. 남자는 그 빈 좌석이 사실은 아내를 위한 것이었지만, 그녀는 죽었다고 대답했다.

대답을 들은, 조는 매우 안타까웠지만, 그 빈 좌석을 왜 가족이나 친척 중 다른 사람에게 주지 않았냐고 물었다. 그가 대답하길, "그러려고 했는데요, 다들 아내의 장례식에 가버렸어요."

06 / 이사 가면 떡부터 돌립시다. 본문 p.22

move into	이사오다
neighborhood	동네
a few	약간
carry	지니다
purse	지갑
find out	알아내다
pass	경과하다
owner	소유자, 주인
rang	ring의 과거 (울리다)
completely	완전히
walk around	주변을 돌아다니다
wonder	이상하게 여기다
stoop	웅크리다
pick up	집어 들다
immediately	즉시
drew	draw의 과거 (빼다)
in horrror	겁에 질려
cockroaches	바퀴벌레
an army of	~의 떼
skeleton	해골

정답

1. neighborhood - 동네
   accident - 사고
   skeleton - 해골
2. cockroaches
3. ①

2. cockroaches

마침내, 집주인은 바퀴벌레 떼로 덮여있는 아기를 발견했다.

3. ①

본문에 의하면 거의 없는 정도가 아니라 아는 사람이 없다고 했다.

해석

일본에서, 한 젊은 여자와 그녀의 아기가 한 집으로 이사 왔다. 그들은 이 동네에 처음이어서, 아무도 아는 사람이 없었다. 이사 오고 며칠이 지난 후, 그 엄마는 자동차 사고로 죽었다. 그 당시 그녀가 지갑을 가지고 있지 않았기 때문에, 그녀가 누구인지 아무도 알지 못했다.

몇 달이 지났다. 그 엄마가 살던 집의 주인이 와서 벨을 눌렀다. 대답이 없어서, 잠시 기다린 후에, 그는 자신이 가지고 있는 열쇠로 문을 열었다. 집은 완전히 어두웠다. 그는 젊은 엄마의 이름을 부르며 돌아다녔다. 거실에서 그는 멈춰 섰다. 마루에는 작고 까만 인형이 하나 있었다. 그는 이 인형이 여기에 왜 있는지 궁금했다. 그는 인형을 들기 위해 웅크렸지만, 즉시 공포로 가득 차 손을 빼버렸다. 그것은 검은색 인형이 아니었다. 그것은 인간 아기의 해골에 있던 바퀴벌레 뭉텅이였다.

07 / 눈을 기증 받고 그녀는 눈뜬 장님이 됩니다.

본문 p.24

negative	부정적인
hate	싫어하다
except	~을 제외하고
care for	보살피다
donate	기증하다
a pair of	한 쌍의
blind	눈 먼
refuse	거절하다
arrogance	오만함
take care of	돌보다

정답

1. negative - 부정적인
   donate - 기증하다
   arrogance - 오만함
2. boyfriend
3. ③

2. boyfriend

사실, 그녀에게 눈을 기증한 사람은 그녀의 <u>남자친구</u>였다.

3. ③

소녀의 남자친구는 원래부터 장님이었던 것이 아니고 소녀에게 눈을 줬기 때문에 장님이 됐다.

해석

장님이었기 때문에 불행했던 한 소녀가 있었다. 그녀는 항상 부정적이었다. 그녀는 그녀의 남자친구를 제외한 모든 것과 모두를 싫어했다. 그녀의 남자친구는 항상 그녀의 옆에 있으며 그녀를 매우 많이 보살펴주었다. 어느 날, 그는 그녀에게 그와 결혼해달라고 청혼했다. 하지만 그녀는 말했다. "만약 내가 세상을 볼 수 있게 된다면, 너와 결혼할게."

시간이 지났고, 누군가가 그녀에게 한 쌍의 눈을 기부했다. 그래서 그녀는 모든 것을 볼 수 있게 되었다. 다시 한번, 그녀의 남자친구는 그녀에게 결혼해달라고 했다. 그녀가 그를 봤을 때, 그녀는 그 또한 장님이었다는 것을 알 수 있었다. 그녀는 오만하게 거절했다. 그는 슬퍼하며 떠났고 나중에 그녀에게 짧은 메시지를 남겼다. "내 눈을 잘 돌봐줘, 자기야."

08 / 겨울잠을 자지 않고 야행성인 곰이 있다고요?

본문 p.26

sun bear	태양 곰
in fact	사실은
smallest	가장 작은
nocturnal	야행성의
during	~동안
rest	쉬다
almost	거의
diet	식사, 식단
consist of	~로 구성되다
insect	곤충
root	(식물) 뿌리
cartoon	만화
unique	독특한
marking	반점
perhaps	아마도
reason	이유

정답

1. (a) 야행성의, (b) 구성되다 **2.** 태양곰
3. ③

1. (a) 야행성의

바로 이어서 (a)에 대한 설명이 나온다. 'nocturnal' 이라 는 소리는 'active at night' 즉, '밤에 활동적인' 이라는 의미이므로 '야행성의' 라고 추론해볼 수 있다.

(b) 포함하다

그들의 식사(Their diet)는 곤충, 과일, 뿌리, 새, 그리고 다른 작은 동물들을 _______한다. 여기에 적절한 것은 '포함하다, 구성되다' 정도로 추론할 수 있다.

2. 태양곰

바로 앞문장의 sun bear를 받는다.

3. ③

① 겨울잠에 대한 언급은 없다.
② 야행성이라고 나온다.
④ 만화에서처럼 꿀을 좋아한다.
⑤ 무늬 때문에 지어진 이름일 거라고 알려져 있다.

해석

곰들은 보통 매우 크다. 그러나, 몇몇 곰들은 작다. 태양곰은 작은 곰이다. 사실 이것은 곰 중에 가장 작은 종류의 곰이다. 태양곰들은 야행성이다. 즉, 그들은 주로 밤에 활발하다. 낮에는 나무 위에서 휴식을 취한다. 그들은 거의 어떤 것이든 먹을 수 있다. 그들의 식사는 곤충, 과일, 뿌리, 새, 그리고 다른 작은 동물들로 구성된다. 만화 속의 곰들처럼, 태양곰은 꿀을 좋아한다. 태양곰은 뜨고 있는 해처럼 보이는 무늬를 가지고 있다. 아마도 이것이 태양곰이라고 불리는 이유일 것이다.

section 3

09 / 자, 지금부터 방 번호를 알아보도록 하지

본문 p.30

just before	바로 전에
fell asleep	fall sleep의 과거 (잠들다)
realize	깨닫다
parking lot	물건
stuff	잠그다
lock	단지
only	기억하다
remember	잠시
for a while	열다
unlock	울리다
honk	경적
horn	켜다
turn on	기억하다

정답

1. realize – 깨닫다
   parking lot – 주차장
   remember – 기억하다
2. 경적을 울리다
3. ④

2. 경적을 울리다
   시동도 걸지 않은 채로 운전자석에 앉았다는 것이 첫 번째 힌트가 될 수 있고, 그 뒷문장에 호텔에 있는 모든 방이 불을 켜기 시작했다는 것은 두 번째 힌트가 될 수 있다.

3. ④ 잘 들리지 않는 사람이 자신의 방을 찾는 방법
   ① 잘 자는 방법
   ② 잘 들리지 않는 사람을 돕는 방법
   ③ 차를 더 잘 주차하는 방법
   ⑤ 잘 기억하는 방법

해석

두 친구는 귀가 잘 들리지 않았다. 그들은 함께 여행하고 있었는데 어두워져 호텔에 갔다. 막 잠들기 전에, 친구 중 하나가 차에 무언가 놓고 왔다는 것을 깨달았다. 그는 주차장에 있는 자신의 차에 갔다. 물건을 꺼낸 후, 그는 차를 잠갔는데, 방 번호가 기억나지 않는다는 것을 깨달았다.

잠시 생각하니 좋은 생각이 났다. 그는 차를 다시 열고 운전자석에 앉아서 경적을 울리기 시작했다. 곧, 호텔에 있는 모든 방에서 불이 켜지기 시작했다. 모든 방이 그랬다, 딱 한 방만 빼고.

10 / 21세기에 살고 있어서 다행이야

본문 p.32

law	법
make sense	타당하다
example	예
strange	이상한
in the past	과거에
century	세기
on purpose	일부러
build	짓다
have to	~해야만 하다
pay	지불하다
tax	세금
female	여성
allow	허용하다
get into	~을 (시작)하다
relationship	(연인) 관계
date	데이트하다
be fired	해고 당하다

정답

1. strange - 이상한
   tax - 세금
   allow - 허락하다
2. (a) 창문마다 세금을 붙였기 때문이다,
   (b) 연애를 하는 것 (결혼하거나)

해석

법이 항상 이치에 맞는 것은 아니다. 여기 과거에 이상했던 법의 몇몇 예가 있다.

영국의 18세기에, 가난한 사람들은 고의적으로 창문이 없는 집에 살았다. 그들은 창문을 만들지 않았다, 왜냐하면 그들은 집에 있는 모든 창문에 대해 세금을 내야 했기 때문이다. 만약 당신이 영국 시골 지역에 간다면, 여전히 창문이 없는 집들을 볼 수 있다.

미국의 19세기에, 여자 교사들은 이성과 교제하는 것이 허용되지 않았다. 만약 그들이 결혼을 하거나 데이트하는 것을 선택한다면, 그들은 해고되었다.

11 / 넌 모쏠이었고 21살까지 모쏠이면...

본문 p.34

get out	나가다
fairy	요정
became	become의 과거 (~이 되다)
curse	저주하다
beast	짐승
once upon a time	옛날 옛날에
far away	아주 먼
castle	성
arrogant	오만한
knock	두드리다
beg	구걸하다
stay	머물다
until	~때까지
someone	누군가
truly	진정으로
remain	남다
refuse	거부하다

정답

1. refuse - 거절하다
   arrogant - 오만한
   beg - 구걸하다
2. (B) – (A) – (C)
3. ⑤

2. (B) – (A) – (C)

'그러나' 로 시작하는 (A)보다, '옛날 옛적에' 로 시작하는 것이 더 적절하다. (B) 마지막은 늙고 불쌍한 여인이 하룻밤 묵는 것을 부탁했다고 하니, 거절했다는 내용으로 시작하는

(A)가 적절하다. 그리고 마지막으로 남은 것은 (C) 하나이다.

3. ⑤

왕자는 잘못을 뉘우칠 때까지 야수로 살아야 되는 것이 아니고 그를 진정으로 사랑해줄 여자를 찾을 때까지 야수로 살아야 한다.

해석

(B) 옛날 옛날에, 아주 멀리에 있는 왕국에, 산꼭대기에 아름다운 성이 있었다. 성 안에는 젊고 잘 생겼지만 매우 오만한 왕자가 살고 있었다. 어느 매우 추운 날, 한 늙고 불쌍한 여자가 성문을 두들겼다. 그녀는 젊은 왕자에게 하룻밤 묵을 장소를 구걸했다.
(A) 하지만, 왕자는 거절했고, 그녀에게 나가라고 말했다. 그러자 그 늙은 여자는 요정으로 변했다. 그리고 나서 그녀는 왕자를 야수가 되도록 저주를 걸었다.
(C) 그녀는 그에서 장미 한 송이를 주고 그에게 이 장미는 왕자의 스물 한살 생일까지 살 것이라고 말했다. 만약 그가 그때까지 진정으로 그를 사랑해줄 누군가를 찾지 못한다면, 그는 죽는 날까지 야수로 남을 것이다.

12 / 꿀잼 나라의 흔한 헤어 살롱 본문 p.36

hair salon	미용실
wait	기다리다
hairdresser	미용사
come back	돌아오다
excellent	훌륭한
forgot	forget의 과거 (잊다)
met	meet의 과거 (만나다)
grab	붙잡다

정답

1. ① 남자

2. ⑤

3. ① 화난

1. ① 남자

2. ⑤ 소년이 남자와 오늘 처음 만난 사이라는 것을 미용사에게 말한다.

① 소년은 아빠가 아닌 오늘 처음 만난 남자와 미용실에 갔다.

② 남자가 먼저 머리를 했다.

③ 남자는 잠시 전화를 하고 온다며 나갔지만 돌아오지 않았다.

④ 머리 비용은 본문에 언급되어있지 않다.

3. ① 화난

사기 당했다는 것을 깨닫는 순간이기 때문에, 본문에서는 'upset' 이 가장 적절하다

② 신난 ③ 행복한

④ 재미있는 ⑤ 만족스러운

4. 예시답안) 경찰에 신고한다, 소년의 부모님한테 연락한다. 등등 내용에 잘 이어지는 선에서 자유롭게 쓰면 OK!

해석

한 남자와 소년이 미용실에 들어왔다. 소년은 남자가 먼저 머리를 하는 동안 기다렸다. 그가 끝나자, 남자는 소년을 데려다 의자 위에 앉혀 놓았다. 남자는 미용사에게 애한테 멋지게 머리를 해주라고 말했다. 그리고 나서, 그는 소년에게 전화 좀 하고 온다고 말했다. 미용사는 소년의 머리를 멋지게 잘랐지만, 남자는 돌아오지 않았다.

오랜 시간을 기다린 후, 미용사는 소년에게 말했다. "내 생각에 너희 아버지께서는 너를 잊으신 것 같구나. 나는 그가 약간 걱정이 되네." 하지만 소년은 대답했다. "그 사람은 저희 아버지가 아닌데요? 우리는 오늘 아침에 만났어요. 그는 제 손을 잡고, 우리는 공짜로 머리를 하러 갈 거라고 말했어요."

section 4

13 / 이승 탈출 넘버원 - 위험한 편지 봉투 본문 p.40

post office	우체국
grandparent	조부모
envelope	봉투
glue	풀
lick	핥다
shut	닫다
tight	단단한
brush	닦다
lump	혹
tongue	혀
hurt	아프다
examine	검사하다
cockroach	바퀴벌레
climb out	기어나오다
cut open	절개하다
enter	들어가다
warm	따뜻한
moist	촉촉한
hatch	부화시키다

정답

1. lick – 핥다
lump – 혹
hatch – 부화하다

2. 바퀴벌레 **3.** warm, moist

3. warm, moist

질문: 어떻게 바퀴벌레 알들이 그의 혀 안쪽에서 부화하고 자랄 수 있었을까?
답변: <u>따뜻하고</u> <u>촉촉했기</u> 때문에

해석

한 젊은 남자가 우체국에 있었다. 그는 멀리 사는 조부모님께 편지를 썼었다. 그는 봉투 안에 편지를 넣었지만, 풀을 가지고 있지 않았다. 그는 봉투를 핥고 단단히 닫았다. 그가 편지를 보내고 며칠 후, 그가 혀에 혹을 본 것은 이를 닦고 있을 때였다. 아파지기 시작하자, 그 다음날 그는 병원에 갔다.

그를 검사한 후에, 의사는 혹을 잘라 열었는데, 거기서 바퀴벌레 한 마리가 기어 나왔다. 봉투 일부분에 바퀴벌레 알이 있었던 것이다. 그가 봉투를 핥았을 때, 그는 혀를 베었고, 그래서 알들이 혀로 들어간 것이다. 따뜻하고 촉촉했기 때문에, 알들은 그의 혀 안에서 부화할 수 있었고, 크기가 커졌다. 이것이 바로 당신이 항상 조심해야 하는 이유이다.

14 / 사랑과 전쟁 - 못된 남편과 못 박는 아내

본문 p.42

temper	기질
beat	때리다
drunk	취한
regret	후회하다
realize	깨닫다
last longer	오래 지속되다
forgiveness	용서
whenever	~ 할 때마다
hammer	망치질하다
nail	못
living room	거실
decide	결심하다
suggest	제안하다
agree	동의하다
as time went by	시간이 지남에 따라
disappear	사라지다
leave	떠나다
shock	충격을 주다
thought	think의 과거 (생각하다)
look at	보다
even though	~에도 불구하고
remove	제거하다
wound	상처

정답

1. regret – 후회하다
   last – 지속되다
   hammer – 망치질하다
2. disappeared
3. 상처는 여전히 남아있기 때문에
4. ⑤

2. disappeared

was removed는 '제거되었다' 라는 뜻인데, 그 문장 전체 (Even though every nail was removed, the wounds are still there.)를 해석해보면 '비록 모든 못이 제거되었을지라도, 상처는 여전히 남아있다.' 라고 해석이 된다. 이것을 disappeared로 교체하면, '비록 모든 못이 사라졌을지라도,' 로 해석이 어색하지 않다.

3. 상처는 여전히 남아있기 때문에

아내는 자신의 상처를 못에 비유하는데, 이는 결국 지금 Peter가 아내한테 잘하려고 노력할지라도 이미 받은 상처는 치유가 어렵다는 것을 의미한다.

4. ⑤

그가 더 이상 이성을 잃지 않게 된 것은 맞으나 아내는 그를 떠나려고 했다.

해석

피터는 나쁜 기질들을 가지고 있었다. 그는 쉽게 화를 냈다. 그는 심지어 술을 마시면 아내를 때리기도 했다. 그가 이성을 잃은 다음날이면, 그는 항상 후회하고, 얼마나 어리석었는지에 대해 깨달았다. 하지만 오래 지속되지는 않았다.

어느 날 아침, 그가 용서를 구하는 동안, 그의 아내는 울고 있었다. 그녀는 그에게 말했다. "당신이 이성을 잃을 때마다, 나는 거실 벽에 못을 박을거야."

한 달 동안, 그녀는 28개의 못을 박았다. 그는 마침내 거실이 얼마나 흉한지 깨달았다. 그래서 그는 바뀌기로 결심했고, 정말로 바뀌었다. 그녀는 매일매일 점점 덜 못질하게 되었다. 마침내 그는 전혀 이성을 잃지 않게 되었다. 그는 심지어 아내에게 만약 그녀에게 잘하면, 못들을 하나씩 뽑을 것을 제안했고, 그녀는 동의했다.

시간이 지남에 따라, 벽에 있는 못들이 사라져버렸다. 하지만, 어느 날, 그녀는 그에게 말했다. "나, 당신을 떠날 거야. 잘 지내, 피터." 그는 충격 받았다. "오, 안돼, 여보, 난 내가 잘해오고 있다고 생각했는데, 난 이제 달라졌어, 당신이 잘 알잖아." "맞아, 피터. 하지만, 벽을 봐. 대부분의 못이 없어지긴 했지만, 상처들은 여전히 남아있어." 라고 아내가 대답했다.

15 / 이런 놈도 여자친구가 있는데... 본문 p.46

bump	쿵!
flat tire	바람 빠진 타이어
pull over	길 한쪽에 차를 대다
driving	운전
sympathetic	동조하는
terrible	끔찍한
actually	실제로
wrong	잘못된

정답

1. ③ **2.** ③

3. 바람이 빠진 타이어를 교체한 것이 아닌 멀쩡한 타이어를 교체해서

1. ③

만약 sympathetic의 뜻을 알았다면 바로 답을 골랐겠지만, 몰랐다면 한번 추론을 해보자. 이 단어 앞 문장을 보면 남자가 데이트에 늦은 이유를 설명하고, 그 뒷문장에서는 그녀가 맞장구 쳐주는 내용이 나오는 것으로 봐서는 그녀가 '동조하고' 있다고 추론해볼 수 있다.

2. ③

여자 친구는 도로가 끔찍해서 그랬을 거라고 생각했다.

해석

한 남자가 여자친구와의 데이트에 늦었다. 그는 그녀에게 그가 늦은 데에는 이유가 있다고 말했다. "내가 크게 '펑' 하는 소리를 들었을 때, 이쪽으로 운전하면서 오는 중이었거든. 그리고 쿵 쿵 쿵 소리가 나는 거야. 나는 바로 바퀴에 바람이 빠졌다는 것을 알았지. 그래서 길 옆에 차를 세우고 타이어를 바꿨어. 근데 내가 다시 운전을 시작했을 때, 나는 또 다시 쿵 쿵 쿵 소리를 듣기 시작하는 거야!" 그의 여자친구는 동조해줬다. "도로가 정말 끔찍했구나! 다른 바퀴도 바람이 빠진 거야?" "사실은, 아니." 남자는 대답했다. "그저 잘못된(바람이 안 빠진) 타이어를 바꿔 꼈던거야."

16 / 돌고래는 옛날에는 육지에서 살았던 것 같아요. 본문 p.48

dolphin	돌고래
gill	아가미
breathe	호흡하다
underwater	물속에서
tail	꼬리
leap	치솟다
definitely	분명히

정답

1. gills **2.** ⑤

1. gills

> 물고기들은 아가미를 가지고 있기 때문에,
> 그들은 물 속에서도 숨쉴 수 있다.

2. ⑤

본문의 'They are actually quite different from fish.' 라는 문장을 통해 돌고래는 물고기와 다르다는 것을 분명히 하고 있다.

해석

몇몇 사람들은 돌고래가 물고기라고 생각하지만, 그들은 사실 물고기와는 다르다. 물고기는 물 아래서 숨쉬기 위해 아가미를 가지고 있지만, 돌고래는 아가미를 가지지 않는다. 대신에, 돌고래들은 인간이 하는 것처럼 공기로 숨을 쉴 필요가 있다. 또한 물고기는 수영을 할 때, 꼬리를 좌우로 흔들지만, 돌고래는 꼬리를 위아래로 움직인다. 돌고래는 하늘로 치솟기 위해 꼬리를 사용한다. 돌고래는 분명히 물고기는 아니다, 비록 그들과 비슷하게 생기긴 했지만.

section 5

17 / 손님들 스케줄에 맞춰서 파티를 열도록 하죠.

본문 p.52

husband	남편
invite	초대하다
force	강요하다
unfortunate	유감스러운
fortunate	운이 좋은
amazing	놀라운

정답

1. ② 2. free 3. ⑤

1. ② 유감스러운, 불운한

본문에서 남편은 아내의 친구들에게 계속 매일의 일정을 묻다가 친구들이 안 된다고 하는 날이 나오니 안타까워하며 그날 초대하려고 했다고 말하고 있다. 따라서 안타까워하는 것과 관련된 단어를 고르면 되는데 unfortunate가 가장 적절하다.

① 행복한 ③ 운 좋은, 다행한

④ 놀라운 ⑤ 운 좋은

2. free

질문: 아내의 친구들을 초대하지 않기 위한 그의 계획은 무엇이었나요?
대답: 그의 계획은 그들이 시간이 없을 때까지 시간이 있는지를 계속해서 묻는 것이었습니다.

3. ⑤

스케줄이 우연히 겹친 것이 아니라 남자가 아내 친구들의 스케줄이 겹칠 때까지 계속 물었다.

해석

한 여자가 남편한테 파티를 위해 집으로 그녀의 친구들을 부르라고 했다. 남편은 아내의 친구들을 초대하고 싶지 않았지만, 그녀의 아내는 그가 친구들을 어쨌든 부르도록 강요했다. 그는 아내의 친구들에게 내일 무엇을 할 것이냐고 물었다. 그들은 그에게 아무것도 안 한다고 말했다. 그는 그 리고 나서 그 다음날은 무엇을 할 것이냐고 물었다. 그들은 그날 역시 아무것도 안 한다고 말했다. 그는 또 그 그 다음날은 무엇을 할 것이냐고 묻자, 그들은 그날 여행을 갈 것이라고 대답했다. 남자는 그리고 대답했다. "아 저런! 정말 안타깝네요! 제가 그날 집에 초대하려고 했는데요!"

18 / 상위 1%만 흑백 TV를 가질 수 있었다죠?

본문 p.54

invent	발명하다
show	보여주다
air	방송하다
develop	발달하다
sold	sell의 과거분사 (팔다)
nowadays	오늘날
high-definition	고화질

정답

1. invent – 발명하다
   air – 방송하다
   expensive – 비싼
2. 고화질 3. ①,④

2. 고화질

바로 뒷문장을 보면 '많은 컬러와 선명한 이미지들을 보여줄 수 있다' 라는 문장과 연결하여 '고화질' 이라고 추론해 볼 수 있다.

3. ①, ④

① TV는 1925년에 처음으로 발명되었다.

④ 본문에 1953년 컬러 TV가 개발되어 판매되었다고 나와 있다.

해석

첫 텔레비전은 1925년 존 베어드에 의해서 발명되었다. 이것은 한 색만을 가졌고 인간의 얼굴 사이즈쯤 됐다.

첫 텔레비전 방송국은 1928년 뉴욕에 세워졌다. 아주 적은 수의 사람들만이 텔레비전을 가질 수 있었다. 텔레비전은 오직 하루에 두 시간만 보여졌다.

1948년 미국에는 4개의 큰 텔레비전 방송국이 있었다. 이들은 밤 8시부터 11시까지 하루에 세 시간씩 쇼를 방영했다. 텔레비전이 항상 오늘날 그런 것과 같은 것을 보여주던 것은 아니었다.

1953년에는 컬러 텔레비전이 마침내 개발되어 팔렸다. 그러나 그것들은 종종 대부분의 사람들에게 너무 비쌌다. 방송은 여전히 흑백으로 보여졌다.

오늘날 대부분의 텔레비전은 (a)고화질로 시청된다. 그것은 텔레비전이 많은 라인들을 가진다는 것을 의미하는데, 그래서 그것들은 많은 컬러와 선명한 이미지들을 보여줄 수 있다. 몇몇의 사람들은 심지어 3-D 텔레비전(3-D로 비디오를 보여주는)까지 집에 가지고 있다.

19 / 사랑의 질주

본문 p.56

frightened	무서운
slow down	늦추다
moreover	게다가
take off	벗다
put ~ on	입다, 쓰다
bug	귀찮게 하다
burst into	~을 터트리다
highway	고속도로
prevent	예방하다
instead of	대신에
hand over	건네다

정답

1. bug – 귀찮게 하다
   suddenly – 갑자기
   prevent – 예방하다
2. scared 3. ④ 4. ③

2. scared

frightened와 scared는 둘 다 '무서워하는, 겁먹은' 이라는 뜻을 갖는다. 문맥에서 봤을 때도, frightened을 포함한 문장에서는 오토바이를 너무 빨리 몰아서 겁먹었다는 내용이고, scared 앞 문장을 포함해서 설명하면 남자친구가 시키는대로 다 했는데도 속도를 줄이지 않아 무섭고 겁먹었다는 것이다.

3. ④

본문에서 남자는 오토바이가 고장 났으며 막을 수 없다는 것까지 인지하고 있다.

4. ③ 죽음보다 강한 사랑

본문은 오토바이나 사고자체 보단 죽음 앞에서 사랑하는 사람을 살리기 위해 희생하는 사랑얘기가 중심이 된다.

① 안전운전의 중요성
② 우리가 오토바이 헬멧을 착용해야 되는 이유
④ 브레이크 고장을 다루는 방법
⑤ 당신의 사랑을 여자친구에게 표현하는 방법

해석

한 젊은 커플이 오토바이를 타고 있었다. 그들은 너무 빨라서, 젊은 여자는 무서웠다. 그녀의 남자친구가 오토바이를 운전하고 있었다. 그녀는 그에게 속도를 낮추라고 했다. 하지만 그는 빠르게 달리는 것이 너무 재미있기 때문에 그렇게 하고 싶지 않다고 말했다.

게다가 그는 그녀에게 성가시니까 자신의 헬멧을 벗겨 그녀의 머리에나 쓰라고 말했다. 그는 만약 그녀가 그렇게 하면, 속도를 낮추겠다고 약속했다. 그래서 그녀는 그의 헬멧을 벗겨 그녀의 머리에 썼지만, 그는 속도를 전혀 낮추지 않았다. 마침내, 그녀는 너무 겁먹어서 눈물을 터뜨렸다. 하지만, 그는 여전히 속도를 낮추지 않았고, 그저 그녀에게 너무 많이 사랑하며 이것을 꼭 기억하라고 말했을 뿐이다.

그날 오후 뉴스에, 고속도로에서 벌어진 오토바이 사고가 하나 있었다. 젊은 커플의 브레이크가 갑자기 작동하지 않았다. 젊은 남자는 그가 사고를 예방할 수 없으리란 것을 알았다. 그는 본인 대신 여자친구를 구하기로 선택했지만, 그는 그녀가 알게 되길 원하지 않았다. 그래서 그는 그가 썼던 헬멧을 넘겨주고 그녀에게 너무 많이 사랑한다고 말했다.

20 / 아휴~ 요즘 누가 애를 직접 기르나요~

본문 p.60

discuss	의논하다
decide	결심하다
farm	농사짓다
adorable	사랑스러운
send	보내다

정답

1. discuss - 의논하다
decide - 결심하다
adorable - 사랑스러운
2. ② **3.** 해설 참고
4. tree, farm, grandparents

1. ②

소년과 소녀는 아이를 낳아 직접 키울 계획이 없고 그들의 조부모님께 보내버릴 계획이다.

3. 예시답안) 아이는 키워주겠지만 용돈은 두둑이 달라고 말한다. 등등 자신의 생각을 자유롭게 쓰면 OK!

4. tree, farm, grandparents

아버지: 너희는 어디에서 살거니?
소년: 우리는 언덕 위의 우리의 나무 집에서 살거예요.
아버지: 음식은 어떻게 얻을거니?
소년: 우리는 우리 집 근처에서 농사지을 거예요.
아버지: 어떻게 아이들을 기를 거니?
소년: 우리는 애들을 그들의 조부모님에게 보낼거예요.

해석

한 어린 소년과 소녀가 소년의 아버지에게 그들이 결혼할 거라고 말했다. 아버지는 그의 아들에게 그와 아내가 어디서 살 것이냐고 물었다. 소년은 그와 장차 아내가 될 사람이 이미 그 문제에 대해서 상의를 했으며, 그들은 언덕 위에 나무 집을 짓기로 결심했다고 말했다.

소년의 아버지는 그리고 어떻게 음식과 물을 위한 돈을 얻을 것이냐고 물었다. 그 소년은 또다시 그와 장차 아내가 될 사람이 이미 그 문제에 대해서 상의를 했으며 그들은 그들의 나무 집 근처에서 농사를 지을 계획이라 돈이 많이 필요하지 않을 것이라고 말했다. 사랑스럽다고 느낀, 소년의 아버지는 그들이 아이를 가질 것인지를 물었다. 소년은 그들은 또한 아이들을 가질 계획이며, 일단 아이들이 생기게 되면 그들을 조부모님께 보낼 것이라고 대답했다.

section 6

21 / 에디슨, 그는 이미 전설이었다 본문 p.66

inventor	발명가
determination	결단력
light bulb	전구
learn	배우다

정답

1. determination - 결단력
   invent - 발명하다
   fail - 실패하다
2. ⑤

2. ⑤ 그는 가끔은 쉽게 포기하는 남자였다.
   본문에서 에디슨은 무언가를 하려고 결심하면,
   그는 반드시 했다고 나와있다.

   ① 그는 위대한 발명가였다.
   ② 그는 계획을 행동에 옮기는 남자였다.
   ③ 그는 전구를 발명했다.
   ④ 전구는 천 번도 넘는 시도 후에 발명되었다.

해석

토마스 에디슨(Thomas Edison)은 단순히 위대한 발명가가 아니다. 그는 강철과 같은 결의에 찬 남자였다. 만약 무언가를 하려고 결심하면, 그는 그것을 했다. 그것이 어떻게 그가 전구를 발명했는지를 말해준다. 한번은, 누군가 그에게 물었다, "나는 당신이 천 번도 넘게 전구를 만들려고 시도했는데, 항상 실패했다고 들었소. 그렇게 많이 실패하면 기분이 어때요?" 에디슨이 대답했다, "나는 전구를 만드는 천 번의 잘못된 방법을 배운 것이지 실패하지 않았소."

22 / 모두를 벌벌 떨게 만드는 시카고 폭주족의 위엄

본문 p.68

tough	거친
left	leave의 과거 (떠나다)
bar	술집
stolen	훔쳐진
order	주문하다
a shot of whiskey	위스키 한 잔
shout	외치다
by the time	~할 때까지
happen	일어나다
as well	~도 또한
as soon as	~하자마자
report	보고하다
bartender	바텐더
casually	무심코
on foot	걸어서

정답

1. order - 주문하다
   casually - 무심코
   on foot - 걸어서
2. 호텔에 걸어서 돌아갔을 것이다.

해석

한 거친 폭주족이 자신의 오토바이가 도난 당했다는 것을 발견하고 술집을 떠났다. 화가 난, 그는 다시 술집으로 돌아와서 위스키 한 잔을 주문했다. 그가 소리치길, "만약 내 오토바이가 이 위스키가 끝날 때까지 돌아오지 않는다면, 어제 시카고에서 일어난 일이 여기서도 일어날 거야!" 많은 사람들이 두려움에 술집을 떠나 그의 오토바이를 찾기 시작했다.

그 폭주족이 떠나려고 일어나자마자, 한 남자가 술집으로 들어와 보고했다. "당신의 오토바이가 돌아왔어요!" 폭주족이

막 술집을 떠나려 할 때, 바텐더는 시카고에서 일어났던 일이 무엇인지 물었다. 그는 무심히 대답했다. “호텔에 걸어서 갔죠.”

23 / 세상에 진짜 공짜는 없다니 본문 p.70

wish	바라다
anonymously	익명으로
fabulous	끝내주는, 환상적인
mailbox	우편함

정답

1. 익명으로 2. ③ 3. ④

1. 익명으로

만약 당신이 편지를 “익명으로” 쓴다면, 그것은 당신이 누구인지에 대해서 쓰지 않는 것을 의미한다.

2. ③ 멋진, 훌륭한

(b)fabulous라는 단어는 ‘환상적인, 엄청난’이라는 뜻이다. 만약 이 단어의 뜻을 몰랐다고 할지라도 문맥상 제임스는 영화를 보러 가는 것이 소원일 정도였는데 돈이 없어서 볼 수 없었는데 누군가 티켓을 줘서 고대하던 영화를 보러 갔다 왔으니 멋진 시간을 보냈을 것이라고 추론해볼 수도 있다.

① 실망스러운 ② 슬픈
④ 웃기는 ⑤ 짜증나는

3. ④ 충격 받은

우편함에 있던 편지의 내용은 James에게 티켓을 준 사람이 쓴 편지이며 제임스가 영화를 보러 간 동안 제임스의 컴퓨터를 훔쳐갔다는 내용이므로, ‘충격 받았을’ 가능성이 가장 높다.

① 감사하는 ② 행복한
③ 피곤한 ⑤ 만족스러운

해석

제임스는 소원이 하나 있었다. 그는 영화를 보러 가고 싶었다. 그러나 그는 돈이 없었다. 그는 매우 슬펐다.

어느 날, 그는 반가운 뜻밖의 소식을 접했다. 누군가 그에게 티켓 한 장을 익명으로 보낸 것이다. 그는 그가 아는 모든 사람에게 그들이 이것을 보냈냐고 물었지만, 그들은 아니라고 말했다. 제임스는 어찌됐건 영화를 보러 갔다. 그는 멋진 시간을 보냈다.

그가 집에 돌아왔을 때, 그는 우편함에 있는 편지 한 통을 발견했다. 그는 그것을 열었는데, 거기에는 “영화 재미있었니? 잘됐군! 어쨌든, 네가 나한테 티켓 값을 빚졌으니, 난 너의 컴퓨터를 가져간다~! 세상에 공짜는 없지, 안 그래?

24 / 물건은 만드는 게 아니고 파는 것이다

본문 p.72

perfume	향수
hit the market	출시하다
market	시장
be able to	~할 수 있다
prestigious	명성이 높은
cosmetic	화장품
exhibit	전시회, 시연회
spill	엎지르다
crowd	군중
scent	냄새

정답

1. hit the market – 출시하다
spill – 엎지르다
scent – 냄새
2. 고의로 3. ② 4. ③

2. 고의로

바로 앞에 'hiding her intention' 즉 '그녀의 의도를 숨긴채' 라는 표현을 통해 '고의로' 엎질렀다는 것을 추론할 수 있다.

3. ②

이 글은 전반적으로 에스티 로더의 마케팅 전략에 초점이 맞춰져 있다.

4. ③

본문에 보면 영국에서 잘 팔렸음에도 불구하고 파리에 있는 명품관에는 입점할 수가 없었다고 나와있다.

해석

1953년 에스티 로더(Estee Lauder)의 첫 번째 향수 "Youth Dew"가 출시되었다. 비록 그것이 런던에서 잘 팔렸을지라도, 그녀는 그것을 팔도록 파리에 있는 명품관에는 입점할 수 없었다.

파리에 있는 중요한 화장품 시연회를 하는 동안, 그녀의 의도를 숨기고, 에스티는 "고의적으로" 그녀의 Youth Dew 병을 사람들 한 가운데서 엎질렀다. 향기는 빠르게 퍼졌고 많은 고객들은 그녀의 상품에 관심을 가지게 되었다.

사람들은 또한 사지 않더라도 가게에서 그녀의 향수를 뿌려볼 수 있었다. 그녀의 영리한 마케팅 기술 덕택에, 에스티 로더는 성공적인 화장품 회사를 세울 수 있었다.

25 / 주인님, 저 여기 있어요... 죄송 본문 p.76

faithful	충실한
slept	sleep의 과거 (자다)
whenever	~할 때는 언제든지
woke up	wake up의 과거 (깨다)
lick	핥다
murder	살인
neighborhood	동네
reassured	안심한

정답

1. faithful - 충실한
lick - 핥다
murder - 살인

2. 안심한 **3.** lick **4.** ③

2. 안심한

본문에 보면 리즈는 한밤중에 깨면, 침대 밑에 손을 떨어뜨려 스팟이 핥아주면 그녀는 안심하고 잠이 들었다. 그날 역시 그녀가 겁이 나서 손을 떨어뜨렸고, 스팟이 핥았다고 생각했으므로 '안심'했을 것이다.

3. lick

살인이 그녀의 동네에서 벌어진 다음날, 스팟이 아닌 다른 무언가가 그녀의 손을 핥았다.

4. ③ 공포

항상 리즈를 안심시키기 위해 그녀의 개가 그녀의 손을 핥았는데, 어느 날 무언가가 그녀를 핥았는데 그게 스팟이 아닌 것이라는 것이 밝혀지고 전날에 살인 사건과 맞물리면서 전체적으로 공포

분위기가 조성되어있다.

① 과학 ② 로맨스

④ 코미디 ⑤ 액션

해석

리즈는 그녀의 충성스런 개 스팟과 함께 홀로 살고 있었다. 스팟은 항상 리즈의 침대 바로 옆 마루에서 잤다. 이렇게 해서, 리즈가 한밤 중에 깰 때마다, 그녀는 그녀의 손을 침대 옆으로 떨어뜨리면 스팟은 항상 그곳에 있곤 했다. 그는 그녀가 안전하다는 것을 알게 하도록 그녀의 손을 핥아주곤 했다. 그러면 리즈는 다시 잠들었다.

어느 날 밤, 리즈는 잠을 잘 수가 없었다. 그녀는 약간 두려움을 느꼈다. 왜냐하면 그녀가 전날 그녀의 동네에서 있었던 살인사건에 대한 기사를 읽었기 때문이었다. 그녀는 스팟이 자고 있는 쪽으로 그녀의 손을 떨어뜨렸다. 항상 그랬듯이, 스팟은 그녀의 손을 핥아주었다. 안심이 된, 리즈는 졸리기 시작했다.

잠들기 바로 직전에, 그녀는 거실 쪽을 쳐다봤다. 놀랍게도, 그녀는 스팟이 그녀를 쳐다보며, 거기에 서있는 것을 봤다. 하지만, 만약 스팟이 계속 거실에 있었다면, 바로 전에 그녀의 손을 핥은 것은 무엇이었을까?

26 / 우주복에 대한 자세한 설명 본문 p.78

astronaut	우주비행사
protection	보호
space suit	우주복
gravity	중력
not ~ at all	전혀~하지 않는
straw	빨대
attached	부착된
feature	특징
miniature	미니어처, 소형
spaceship	우주선
diaper	기저귀

정답

1. astronaut - 우주비행사
gravity - 중력
feature - 특징

2. ④ **3.** 기저귀

2. ④

본문에 보면 우주복 안에 기저귀가 있어서 우주복을 벗지 않고 그냥 해버린다고 나와있다.

3. 기저귀

옷을 벗지 않고 그냥 용변을 봐버릴 수 있도록 해주는 것으로 '기저귀' 를 추론할 수 있다.

해석

우주비행사들은 우주에서 무엇을 입을까? 그들은 우주복을 입는다. 우주복은 우주비행사를 위한 옷과 보호물로써의 역할을 한다. 사람들은 우주복이 입기에 너무 무겁다고 생각한다, 왜냐하면 그것은 약 100kg이나 나가기 때문이다. 그러나 우주에는 중력이 없기 때문에, 사실 우주비행사들에게 전혀 무겁지 않다. 우주복은 매우 많은 특징들을 가지고 있다. 우주비행사들은 우주복의 식량 공급처에 붙어있는 빨대를 통해서 먹고 마실 수 있다. 그리고 만약 화장실에 가고 싶으면, 그들은 우주복을 벗지 않고 그냥 해버린다, 왜냐하면 그들은 항상 기저귀를 차고 있기 때문이다. 어떤 면에서 우주복은 마치 소형 우주선과 같다.

27 / 할아버지의 속마음

본문 p.80

celebrate	축하하다
decide	결정하다
invite	초대하다
fairy	요정
appear	나타나다
faithfully	성실하게
grant a wish	소원을 들어주다
twirl	휘두르다
wand	요술지팡이

정답

1. faithfully - 충실히
   grant - 들어주다
   cautiously - 조심스럽게

2. ② 3. ③

2. ②
글에서 초대하지 않은 요정이 파티에 와서 부부가 깜짝 놀랐다 했으므로 ②번이 본문의 내용과 일치하지 않는다.

3. ③

요정은 이번에는 여자의 남편에게 바라는 것이 무엇이냐고 물었다.

남편이 자신의 소원을 말하는 내용이 뒤에 따라오는 ③번의 위치가 다음 문장이 들어가기에가 알맞다.

해석

한 남자의 60번째 생일이었다. 축하하기 위해, 그와 그의 부인은 파티를 열기로 결정했다. 그들은 친구들과 가족, 이웃들을 초대했지만, 요정은 초대하지 않았다. ① 당신은 상상할 수 있을 것이다. 요정이 거실에 나타났을 때 그들이 얼마나 놀랐을지를! 그 요정은 그들에게 25년 동안 결혼생활을 충실히 해왔기 때문에, 각각에게 소원 하나씩을 들어주겠다고 했다. ② 여자가 말했다. “저희는 여행할 돈이 없었어요. 저의 소원은 전세계를 여행하고 싶어요!” 요정이 지팡이를 빙글빙글 돌리자, 두 개의 비행기 티켓이 여자의 손에 쥐어졌다!

③ 요정은 이번에는 여자의 남편에게 바라는 것이 무엇이냐고 물었다. 그 남자는 잠시 생각하더니, 조심스럽게 말했다. “저는 저보다 30살 어린 여자와 결혼할 수 있으면 좋겠네요.” ④ 요정이 지팡이를 돌리자, 그의 소원 역시 이루어졌다. ⑤ 60살 생일에, 그는 90살이 되었다.

28 / 그들 중 누가 집에 갈 수 있었을까 본문 p.82

camping	야영
hiking	하이킹
discover	발견하다
climb up	올라가다
cliff	절벽
laugh	웃다
emerge	나타나다
eventually	결국에
sorrow	슬픔
exactly	정확히
quickly	빨리
arrive	도착하다
astonished	깜짝 놀란
bow	머리를 숙이다
track	흔적
in front of	~의 앞에
tombstone	묘비

정답

1. discover - 발견하다
   emerge - 나타나다
   sorrow - 슬픔
2. ⑤
3. 죽은 것은 그들의 친구가 아니라 네 명의 친구들이었다.

2. ⑤ 깜짝 놀란
astonished의 뜻은 '깜짝 놀란' 이며 이 지문에서는 의미가 shocked와 통한다. astonished의 뜻을 몰랐다면, 문맥을 살펴보자. 죽은 줄 알았던 친구가 일년 전 죽은 장소에 나타난 것을 봤으니 매우 놀라고 충격적이었을 것이다.
① 피곤한 ② 감동한
③ 안심한 ④ 우울한

3. 죽은 것은 그들의 친구가 아니라 네 명의 친구들이었다.
그들의 친구 앞에는 그들의 이름이 적혀있는 네 개의 묘비가 있었다.

해석

어느 날, 다섯 명의 친구들이 캠핑을 갔다. 그들이 작은 호수를 발견했을 때는 산에서 하이킹 중 이었다. 매우 더웠기 때문에, 그들은 호수에서 수영을 하기로 결심했다. 잠시 수영을 한 후에, 친구들 중 하나가 암벽을 기어올라 물 속으로 뛰어들었다. 네 명의 친구들은 웃으며 그가 나타나길 기다렸다.

하지만, 친구가 나타나지 않자 그들은 걱정되기 시작했다. 그들은 물속에 뛰어들어 친구를 위해 물을 수색했지만, 그들은 그의 어떤 흔적도 찾을 수 없었다. 그들은 마침내 멈추고 물 밖으로 나왔다. 그들은 큰 슬픔에 잠겼다. 네 명의 친구들은 서로에게 그들이 정확히 일년 뒤에 돌아오리라 약속했다.

그 해는 빠르게 지나갔다. 그 네 명의 친구들은 죽은 친구를 기억하기 위해서 호수로 돌아왔다. 그러나 그들이 호수에 도착했을 때, 그들은 경악했다. 그들의 친구가 그들 앞에 있는 것이었다! 친구는 그들에게 등을 돌리고 서있었다. 그는 머리를 숙이고 있었다. 그들은 매우 흥분해서 그들의 친구를 향해 달려갔다. 그들은 곧 그들이 가던 길을 멈추게 한 무언가를 봤다. 친구 앞에는 그들의 이름이 적혀있는 네 개의 묘비가 있었다.

section 8

29 / 효도 아닌 효도 본문 p.88

elementary school	초등학교
named	이름을 가진
raise	들다
excellent	훌륭한
visit	방문하다

정답

1. glad - 기쁜
   excellent - 훌륭한
   visit - 방문하다
2. 할머니 집에 있는 동안 앤드류가 말썽을 부려서 집으로 가버리길 원했다.

해석

한 초등학교 교사가 그녀의 어린 학생들에게 사람들을 기쁘게 하는 것에 대해 가르치고 있었다. 그녀는 학생들에게 그들이 누군가를 기쁘게 했던 적이 있었는지를 물었다. 앤드류라는 이름을 가진 한 꼬마가 손을 들었다. 저는 어제 할머니를 기쁘게 해드렸어요." 그가 말했다. "정말 훌륭하구나! 어떻게 그렇게 했니?" 선생님이 물었다.

그가 그녀에게 말했다. "저는 어제 할머니 댁에 4시간 동안 있었거든요. 4시간이 지난 후에, 제가 할머니한테 집에 간다고 말하니까. 그녀는 '네가 간다니 기뻐.' 라고 하시던데요?"

30 / 길냥이들에게 잘해줍시다. 본문 p.90

role	역할
ancient	고대의
Egyptian	이집트인
society	사회
once	한 때
wild cat	야생 고양이
grain	곡식
mice	mouse의 복수 (쥐)
close	가까운
consider	여기다
in fact	사실
prohibit	금지하다
harm	해치다
sentence	선고하다
eyebrow	눈썹
grief	슬픔
sign	표시
mourn	애도하다

정답

1. role - 역할
   prohibit - 금지하다
   mourn - 애도하다
2. (1) 고양이가 죽었을 때
   (2) 고양이의 죽음을 애도하기 위해서
3. ④

3. ④
   본문은 고대 이집트 사회에서의 고양이에 관한 이야기만 있을 뿐 개에 대한 언급은 전혀 없다.

해석

고양이는 고대 이집트 사회에서 매우 중요한 역할을 했다. 한때, 야생 고양이들은 훌륭한 사냥꾼들이었기 때문에, 그들은 굶주린 쥐들로부터 이집트 곡식 창고들을 보호할 수 있었다. 그래서 이집트인들과 고양이들은 매우 가까워졌다. 이집트인들은 고양이를 매우 중요하게 여겨서, 사실, 고양이에게 해를 끼치거나 죽이는 것을 금지하는 법도 있었다! 사람들은 고양이를 죽이면 사형에 처해질 수도 있었다. 고양이가 죽으면, 장례식도 치렀다. 사람들은 눈썹을 밀었는데, 이것은 슬픔의 상징이었으며, 그들 고양이의 죽음을 애도했다.

31 / 두뇌 풀가동하고 수수께끼 시작! 본문 p.92

shot	쏘다, 찍다
dip	담그다
hung up	hang up 과거형 (걸다)
take a picture	사진을 찍다
flesh	살
feather	깃털
scale	비늘
trip over	전복되다
wet	젖은
go up	오르다
come down	내리다
butter	버터

질문 해석

1. 한 남자가 그의 아내를 쏴서, 물에 담그고, 걸어 버렸다. 그리고 다음 날 아침 그들은 훌륭한 아침을 함께 했다. 어떻게?
2. 나는 살도, 깃털도, 비늘이나 뼈도 없다. 하지만 나는 손가락은 있다. 내가 누구게?
3. 네 명의 남자가 보트에 있었다. 그 보트는 전복됐는데, 단 한 명의(single) 남자도 물에 젖지 않았다. 어떻게?
4. 아침으로 절대 절대 먹을 수 없는 두 가지 것은?
5. 오르기만 하고 절대 내려가지 않는 것은?
6. 왜 소년은 그의 창문 밖으로 버터를 던졌는가?

정답 해석

1. 그 남자는 아내의 사진을 찍은 것이다. (현상하기 위해 찍은 사진을) 물에 담그고 (말리기 위해) 걸은 것이다.
   → shoot은 '총을 쏘다' 라는 뜻 이외에도 '사진을 찍다' 라는 뜻이 있다.
2. 장갑
3. 그들은 모두 결혼한 남자기 때문에.
   → 여기서는 single은 '한 명, 한 개' 가 아닌 '미혼' 의 뜻으로 의도했다.
4. 점심과 저녁
5. 당신의 나이
6. 나비가 보고 싶어서
   → 나비는 영어로 butterfly

32 / 부자라서 아내가 예쁜 걸까, 아내가 예뻐서 부자가 된 걸까?

본문 p.94

outline	윤곽
held	hold의 과거분사 (담다)
sauce	소스
president	사장
wear	입다
nightgown	나이트 가운
unique	독특한
success	성공

정답

1. outline – 윤곽
   uique – 독특한
   success – 성공

2. ② 3. 코카콜라 사장 아내의 실루엣

2. ②
   본문은 현재의 코카콜라 병 디자인이 어떻게 만들어지게 됐느냐에 대한 이야기를 하고 있다.

4. 코카콜라 사장 아내의 실루엣
   본문에는 코카콜라 사장이 새로운 병의 디자인을 고심하다 나이트 가운을 입은 아내의 실루엣을 보고 너무 아름다워서 병 디자인으로 적용하게 되었다고 되어있다.

해석

당신은 코카콜라 병이 무엇처럼 보인다고 생각하는가? 병의 윤곽이 어떤 것을 생각나게 하지는 않는가? 오래 전에, 코카콜라가 처음으로 팔렸을 때, 그것은 요리용 소스를 담는 병에 담겼다. 오래지 않아, 코카콜라 사장은 병이 독특해질 필요가 있다고 생각했다. 그는 오래 그리고 골똘히 새로운 병의 디자인에 대해서 생각했지만 그는 어떤 것도 생각해낼 수 없었다. 어느 날 오후, 그는 아내가 나이트 가운을 입고 있는 것을 봤을 때, 여전히 병에 대해서 생각하면서 집에 있었다. 그녀의 몸매의 윤곽은 정말 아름다웠다. 그가 그녀를 보자마자, 사장은 병이 어떻게 보여야 할지 알았다. 그의 병은 엄청난 성공을 거두었다.

section 9

33 / 괘씸하기도 하지만 꽤 재미있는 마케팅 전략

본문 p.98

seem	~로 보이다
cheaper	더 싼
expect	기대하다
deal	거래
department store	백화점
rest room	화장실
usually	보통
several	여러 개의
product	제품
display	진열
prevent	방해하다
hurry	재촉하다
wives	wife의 복수 (아내)
comfortable	편안한
likewise	마찬가지로
grocery store	식료품점
checkout counter	계산대
moreover	더욱이

정답

1. cheap	-	가격이 싼
comfortable	-	편안한
checkout counter	-	계산대
2. ④	3. 해설 참고	

2. ④

본문에는 식료품점이 아니라 백화점에 화장실이 구석에 있다고 언급되어 있다.

3.

1) 패스트푸드 식당에서는 빨리 먹고 빨리 나가도록 딱딱한 의자들로 구성되어 있다.

2) 카페를 지나가면 향기로운 커피 냄새가 새어 나와 들어가고 싶게 한다.

3) 백화점이나 큰 쇼핑몰에서는 고객들이 층층이 구경할 수 있도록 에스컬레이터는 중앙에 있고, 엘리베이터는 구석에 있다.

해석

쇼핑을 할 때, 당신은 쉽게 9,900이나 19,900과 같은 숫자들을 쉽게 볼 수 있다. 이것은 그것들이 10,000이나 20,000보다 훨씬 싸게 보이기 때문이다. 이렇게 하여, 사람들은 그들이 예상한 것보다 더 많이 물건을 사게 된다, 왜냐하면 그들은 좋은 거래를 했다고 느끼기 때문이다.

백화점에서는, 화장실이 보통 각 층의 멀리 떨어진 구석에 있고 심지어 1층에 없기도 하다. 당신은 거기에 가기 위해 길을 벗어나서 가야만 한다. 이렇게 함으로써, 당신은 여러 상품과 진열들을 볼 기회를 가진다.

백화점들은 당신이 시간을 잊고 더 머무를 수 있도록 또한 시계나 창문도 없다. 게다가, 남편이 아내를 재촉하지 못하도록 백화점에는 안락한 의자들이 있다. 이와 마찬가지로 슈퍼마켓이나 식료품 점에서, 계산대에 초콜릿과 캔디바 같은 것들이 있다. 왜냐고? 사람들이 다른 것들에 대해 돈을 지불하고 있을 때 그것들을 살 수 있도록.

34 / 세 가지 흥미로운 역사적 사실들 본문 p.100

historical	역사적인
question	질문
ancient	고대의
ingredient	성분
toothpaste	치약
urine	오줌
Prtuguese	포르투갈인
effective	효과적인
whiten	희게 하다
close to	~에 가까이
understand	이해하다
German	독일어
murder	살해하다
coincidence	우연의 일치

정답

1. ingredient	-	재료
effective	-	효과적인
murder	-	살해하다
2. 우연의 일치		3. ⑤

2. 우연의 일치

애드먼드경을 살해한 범인들의 이름을 합치면 애드먼드경이 살았던 곳 명칭이 되니 이런 '우연의 일치' 가 어딨겠는가.

3. ⑤

애드먼드경을 살해한 범인들의 이름은 Green, Berry, Hill로 동일한 이름은 아니었다.

해석

당신에게 세 개의 흥미로운 역사적 사실에 대해서 질문을 하겠습니다.

1. 고대 로마사람들이 그들의 치약 재료로 썼던 것은 무엇인가요? 바로 인간의 오줌입니다. 심지어 몇몇의 부유한 로마사람들은 포르투갈 남자의 오줌을 사서 그것을 사용했습니다, 왜냐하면 그들은 그것이 이를 하얗게 하는데 더 효과적일 것이라고 생각했기 때문입니다.

2. 알버트 아인슈타인이 죽을 때, 그의 마지막 말은 무엇이었나요? 아무도 그의 마지막 말이 무엇인지 모릅니다, 왜냐하면 그가 무슨 말을 하긴 했는데 그에게 가까이 있던 간호사가 독일어를 몰랐거든요.

3. 1911년에 그린베리 힐의 에드몬드 가드프리 경이 세 명의 남자들에 의해 살해됐습니다. 그들의 이름은 무엇일까요? 그들의 이름은 그린, 베리, 힐이었습니다. 이런 (a)우연의 일치가!

35 / 황금알을 품은 알래스카 본문 p.102

Alaska	알래스카
far from	~로부터 먼
large	큰
one-fifth	5분의 1
covered by	~로 뒤덮힌
glacier	빙하
including	~을 포함하여
environment	환경
explorer	탐험가
trader	상인
sea otter	해달
built	build의 과거분사 (짓다)
therefore	그러므로
million	100만
huge	거대한
cost	비용
per	~당
acre	에어커 (면적의 단위)
in spite of	~에도 불구하고
amazingly	놀랍게도
purchase	사다, 구매하다
resource	자원
salmon	연어
lumber	목재
rich	풍요로운

정답

1. glacier - 빙하
   purchase - 구매하다
   currently - 현재
2. 알래스카를 구매한 것이 실수라 생각해 각종 매체는 구매 결정자였던 슈워드의 이름을 따서 '슈워드의 아이스박스' 라고 별명지었다.
3. ④

2. 알래스카를 구매한 것이 실수라 생각해 각종 매체는 구매 결정자였던 슈워드의 이름을 따서 '슈워드의 아이스박스' 라고 별명지었다.
   슈워드가 정말 저렴한 가격에 알래스카를 구매했음에도 불구하고 그때 당시 많은 미국인들은 그 구매를 실수라고 생각했다.
3. ④
   러시아는 알래스카가 러시아인들이 살기에는 너무 멀다고 판단하여 미국에 팔았다.

해석

알래스카(Alaska)는 미국의 주들 중 하나이다, 하지만 그것은 대부분의 미국 땅에서 멀리 떨어져있다. 알래스카는 미국에서 가장 큰 주이며, 전체 국가의 5분의 1을 차지한다. 이 주는 매우 큰 빙하들과 북아메리카에서 가장 높은 산인, 맥킨리 산을 포함하여 꼭대기가 눈으로 덮여있는 산들로 뒤덮여 있다. 많은 여행객들이 알래스카에서 매년 아름다운 환경에서 하이킹하고 사냥하고 낚시하러 여행을 한다.

러시안 탐험가들은 알래스카를 1741년에 발견했다. 러시아 모피상인들은 곧 해달들을 알래스카 주변 바다에서 사냥하기 시작했다. 그들은 또한 성과 마을을 짓기도 했다. 하지만, 결국 러시아는 알래스카가 러시아 인들이 살기에는 너무 멀다고 판단했다. 그러므로, 러시아는 알래스카를 720만 달러에 1867년 미국에게 팔았다. 이 거대한 주가 에이커(약 1224평)당 단돈 2센트밖에 나가지 않았던 것이다.

이 놀랍도록 싼 가격에도 불구하고, 많은 미국인들은 이 구매가 큰 실수라고 생각했다. 신문들은 이 새로운 지역에 대해 여기를 구입한 국무 장관인 윌리암 H. 수어드의 이름을 따서 "수워드의 아이스박스" 라고 별명 지었다.

하지만 이후의 발견들이 알래스카가 엄청난 자원이라는 것을 입증하였다. 1896년, 금이 이 지역에서 발견돼서, 수천 명이 부자가 되기 위해 알래스카로 이주했다. 이 주는 또한 관광객들이 방문하기에 놀라운 장소일 뿐만 아니라 연어, 목재, 기름의 풍부한 원천이다. 한때 "수어드의 아이스박스" 라고 불렸던 이 주는 현재는 미국의 가장 풍요롭고 아름다운 장소들 중 하나로 꼽힌다.

section 10

36 / 세상은 아직 살만한가 봅니다 본문 p.108

wave	손을 흔들다
none	아무도 ~ 않다
discouraged	낙담한
shabby	초라한
introduce	소개하다
owe	빚지다
pay forward	선행을 베풀다
drove off	drive off의 과거 (떠나다)

잘 이해하고 있나요? p. 109

1. discouraged - 낙담한
   shabby - 남루한
   pay forward - 선행을 베풀다
2. 아무것도 원하지 않았다. 다만 가능하다면 도움이 필요한 사람을 도와주라고 부탁했다.

해석

할머니 한 분이 길가에 서있었다. 그녀는 거기에 서있었는데, 왜냐하면 그녀의 자동차 타이어가 펑크가 났기 때문이었다. 그녀는 지나가는 차들을 향해 손을 흔들었지만, 아무도 멈추지 않았다. 그녀는 낙담하여 손 흔드는 것을 멈췄다.

하지만, 갑자기 차 한대가 그녀 옆에 멈췄다. 그 운전자가 남루했기 때문에, 그녀는 약간 걱정이 되었다. 그는 자신을 제임스 라이언이라고 소개하고 빠르게 할머니의 차에서 펑크 난 타이어를 교체했다. 그가 그의 차로 막 돌아가려고 했을 때, 할머니는 그의 팔을 붙잡았다. "나를 도와준 데에 얼마를 지불해야 하나요?" 그녀가 물었다.

그 남자는 그저 친절하게 웃으며, "만약 저에게 빚졌다고 정말 느껴지신다면, 선행을 베풀어주세요. 도움이 필요한 누군가를 보시면, 저를 생각하고 그 사람을 도와주세요." 그렇게 말하고, 그는 자신의 차로 돌아가서 떠났다.

잘 이해하고 있나요? p. 112

1. 해설 참고 **2.** ③

1. 예시답안) 직접적으로 돈을 주면 사양할 수도 있으므로, 부끄러워서 등등

2. ③

할머니를 도와주었던 someone은 제임스 라이언인데 마지막쯤 여자가 퇴근하고 집으로 돌아와 자고 있는 남편에게 제임스 라이언이라고 부르는 것을 보아 그 둘은 부부 사이라는 것을 알 수 있다.

해석

그날 저녁, 그 할머니는 작은 식당에 들어갔다. 그 식당은 지저분해 보였고 손님도 거의 없었다. 유일한 여종업원이라고는 만삭의 피곤해 보이는 젊은 여성이었다. 그러나 그녀는 친절했고 할머니를 따듯하게 맞이했다.

그 할머니는 그 젊은 여자를 도와야겠다고 결정했다. 그녀는 그 여종업원에게 그녀에게 물을 좀 더 가져다 달라고 부탁했다. 여종업원이 돌아왔을 때, 할머니는 사라진 상태였다. 테이블 위에는 500달러와 메모 하나가 있었는데, 이렇게 적혀있었다. "누군가 나에게 친절을 베풀어 오늘 저를 도왔어요. 저도 선행을 나누고 싶어요. 만약 당신도 가능하다면, 도움이 필요한 사람을 도와 주세요."

그녀가 집에 왔을 때, 그녀의 남편은 이미 자고 있는 중이었다. 그녀는 잠든 남편 옆에 앉아서, 조용히 그에게 할머니와 그녀의 메모에 대해 이야기 했다. 어떻게 그녀가 우리와 곧 태어날 아이를 위해 돈이 필요한지 알았을까. 그녀는 미소 지으며, 코골고 있는 남편에게 속삭였다. "다 잘 될거야. 다 잘 될거야. 사랑해, 제임스 라이언."

종합문제 p. 113

1. ① **2.** ② **3.** ③

1. ① 감동적인

대가를 바라지 않았던 가난한 남자의 따뜻한 선행이 결국 돌아오게 되는 감동적인 이야기이다.

② 낭만적인 ③ 무서운

④ 유머러스 한 ⑤ 재미있는

2. ②

선행이 되돌아오는 이야기이다.

③번의 '뚝배기보다는 장맛이다' 라는 속담은 겉모습으로 모든 것을 판단해서는 안 된다 의미의 속담이다.

3. ③

남자는 금전적인 어떤 대가도 바라지 않았으며 실제로 받지도 않았다.

37 / 판도라의 상자

본문 p.114

revenge	복수
mean	의미하다
stage	단계
lock	잠그다
allow	허락하다
awful	끔찍한
frustrated	좌절한
endure	견디다
hardship	어려움

잘 이해하고 있나요? p. 115

1. 신들로부터 불을 훔쳐, 인간에게 주어서
2. ③

2. ③
판도라는 제우스의 명령으로 헤파이토스가 만들어낸 창조물이다.

해석

제우스는 복수하기로 결심했다. 프로메테우스는 제우스를 매우 화나게 만들었는데, 왜냐하면 그가 신들로부터 불을 훔쳐, 인간에게 주었기 때문이다. 그래서 제우스는 헤파이스토스에게 아름답고 사랑스러운 여자 한 명을 만들어내라고 명령했다, 그리고 그는 그녀에게 판도라라고 이름 지었는데, "온갖 선물들" 이란 뜻이다.

제우스는 그의 계획의 다음 단계를 시작했다. 그는 프로메테우스의 동생인 에피메테우스에게 판도라를 소개해주고 결혼시켰다. 그리고 나서 제우스는 판도라에게 잠긴 작은 상자를 주었다. 그는 에피메테우스에게 이 상자의 열쇠를 주며 그에게 이것을 절대 열어보지 말라고 말했다.

판도라는 매우 그 상자를 열어서 그 안에 무엇이 있는지 알아보고 싶었다. 그러나 에피메테우스는 그녀가 그것을 열어보도록 결코 허락하지 않았다. 어느 날, 에피메테우스가 자는 동안, 그녀는 기회를 봤다. 그녀는 열쇠를 가지고 상자가 잠긴 것을 풀었다.

잘 이해하고 있나요? p. 117

1. ② 2. ②

1. ②
날아다니는 악한 것들을 잡아서 다시 넣으려고 최선을 다했으나, 하나도 건지지 못했으므로 '좌절한' 이 가장 적절하다.

2. ②
증오, 질투, 범죄, 걱정, 질병, 더 많은 끔찍한 것들에 '희망' 을 포함시킨 제우스의 의도를 추론해봐도 정답을 고를 수 있다.
* endure 견디다 | overcome 극복하다 | hardship 고난

해석

판도라가 상자를 열자마자, 끔찍한 것들이 터져 나왔다. 이전에는 존재하지 않았던 증오, 질투, 범죄, 걱정, 질병, 더 많은 끔찍한 것들이 하늘 속으로 날아가 사라져버렸다. 판도라는 날아다니는 악한 것들을 잡아서 다시 집어넣으려고 최선을 다했다. 하지만 그것들은 모두 그녀의 손이 닿지 않는 곳으로 가버렸다. 그녀는 그 상자를 연 것을 얼마나 후회했을까!

판도라는 열린 상자 앞에 털썩 주저앉아 소리지르며 울었다. 좌절하여, 그녀는 다시금 상자를 봤다. 거기 상자 안에는 빛나고 아름다운 무언가가 있었다. 그것은 바로 희망이었다. 제우스는 사람들이 삶의 ⓑ고난들을 ⓐ견디고 극복할 수 있게 희망을 상자 안에 포함시켰다.

종합문제 p. 118

1. ①	2. ④

1. ①

판도라와 결혼한 것은 프로메테우스가 아니고 프로메테우스의 동생 에피메테우스이다.

2. ④

판도라 신화의 내용 자체가 악한 것들이 없는 인간세상에서 판도라가 자신의 호기심 때문에 악한 것들이 담겨있는 상자를 열어 그것들을 세상에 스며들게 하는 내용이다. 이 이야기로부터 하지 말았어야 하는 있을 했을 때 우리는 종종 '판도라의 상자를 열었다' 라는 표현을 사용한다.

무료 다운!
들기 MP3 파일
단어 테스트 생성 프로그램
영작 및 해석 워크북 생성 프로그램
타보름
교육부지정 초등파닉스 영단어800
학습자료 무료다운
한글 발음 쉽게 읽고
그림으로 재미있게!
한글 발음으로 이해가 잘 되는 파닉스 학습
모음이 [A] 하나만 있는 경우나, [A] 뒤로나 함께 이중자음이 될 경우 [애]로 발음한다.
애플 apple
배드 bad
블랙 black
'팩ㅌ fact
피애노ㅜ piano
과 영어발음기호를 동시에
size 'saiz '사이ㅈㅇ
명 크기
What is your shirt size?
셔츠 사이즈가 어떻게 되나요?
small smɔl 'ㅅㅁ(ㅗ)알
형 작은
My shirt size is small.
내 셔츠의 사이즈가 작다.
주변 단어가 반복되는 체계적인 예문
배운 단어를 계속해서 반복
taborm.com

GORiN
GoRee